"Jen Hatmaker works out the glorious equation of God's design for women in her new book, *Ms. Understood*. Not only does she cancel out the misconception that women are second-rate people but she does so with biblical truth, humor, and authenticity. If you are ready to be freed from the 'feminine trend of self loathing,' then Jen's book is just the book for you."

— SUSIE DAVIS, speaker; author of *Loving Your Man Without Losing Your Mind* and *The Time of Your Life*

"So much for my preconceived notion of godly womanhood. Jen Hatmaker has busted those long-cherished myths with solid, biblical truth. Don't miss Jen's witty, hilarious, and highly accurate survey of what's right with women. Forget about the girls in my life—I'm recommending this book to all the guys I know. Here's a picture of womanhood that we all need."

— LAWRENCE W. WILSON, author of *A Different Kind of Crazy: Living the Way Jesus Lived*

"If at all possible, you should invite yourself out to dinner with Jen, because she's smart and funny and godly and warm. That's what I did. If, however, geography or fear of a restraining order prevents that, please read *Ms. Understood*. In it you'll find the same spark, challenge, courage, and belief that Jen carries through life. Her vision for what God can do through women inspires me to live a better, brighter, more fearless life."

— SHAUNA NIEQUIST, author of *Cold Tangerine*

"*Ms. Understood* surprised me. I was expecting a typical book about becoming a woman by God's design. Before I completed the first chapter, I was captivated by the witty, engaging, authentic writing style of Jen Hatmaker. If you are looking for a contemporary understanding of misunderstood women of the Bible (who just might remind you of yourself), read this book. Better yet, gather a group of your favorite friends so you can read and discuss each chapter. You'll laugh out loud, roll on the floor, and find yourself enjoying the study of some pretty intriguing female characters in the Bible. Jen Hatmaker is gifted, smart, and sassy. I love this book!"

— CAROL KENT, speaker; author of *When I Lay My Isaac Down* and *A New Kind of Normal*

JEN HATMAKER

Ms. Understood

Rebuilding the Feminine Equation

NAVPRESS®

For a free catalog
of NavPress books & Bible studies call
1-800-366-7788 (USA) or 1-800-839-4769 (Canada).

www.NavPress.com

The Navigators is an international Christian organization. Our mission is to advance the gospel of Jesus and His kingdom into the nations through spiritual generations of laborers living and discipling among the lost. We see a vital movement of the gospel, fueled by prevailing prayer, flowing freely through relational networks and out into the nations where workers for the kingdom are next door to everywhere.

NavPress is the publishing ministry of The Navigators. The mission of NavPress is to reach, disciple, and equip people to know Christ and make Him known by publishing life-related materials that are biblically rooted and culturally relevant. Our vision is to stimulate spiritual transformation through every product we publish.

ISBN-13: 978-1-60006-216-2
ISBN-10: 1-60006-216-4

Cover design by Charles Brock, The DesignWorks Group, www.thedesignworksgroup.com
Cover image: Veer

Some of the anecdotal illustrations in this book are true to life and are included with the permission of the persons involved. All other illustrations are composites of real situations, and any resemblance to people living or dead is coincidental.

Unless otherwise identified, all Scripture quotations in this publication are taken from the HOLY BIBLE: NEW INTERNATIONAL VERSION® (NIV®). Copyright © 1973, 1978, 1984 by International Bible Society. Used by permission of Zondervan Publishing House. All rights reserved. Other versions used include: the *Contemporary English Version* (CEV). Copyright © 1995 by American Bible Society. Used by permission; *THE MESSAGE* (MSG). Copyright © 1993, 1994, 1995, 1996, 2000, 2001, 2002, 2005. Used by permission of NavPress Publishing Group; the *Holy Bible*, New Living Translation (NLT). Copyright © 1996, 2004. Used by permission of Tyndale House Publishers, Inc., Carol Stream, Illinois 60188. All rights reserved; the New Life Version (NLV). Copyright © 1969 by Christian Literature International; and the King James Version (KJV).

Library of Congress Cataloging-in-Publication Data

Hatmaker, Jen.
   Ms. Understood : rebuilding the feminine equation / Jen Hatmaker.
      p. cm.
   Includes bibliographical references.
   ISBN 978-1-60006-216-2
   1. Women--Religious aspects--Christianity. I. Title.
   BT704.H38 2008
   248.8'43--dc22
                        2008006003
Printed in the United States of America

1 2 3 4 5 6 7 8 / 12 11 10 09 08

This book is dedicated to God, for blessing the world with women. You are the best Creator ever.

Contents

Acknowledgments

How I wish I could name every woman I adore here, but, alas, I'd leave one of you off and have to hear about it later. So I humbly acknowledge the company of women who've spoken wisdom, laughter, inspiration, and holiness into my life. This book is not worthy of you, but you inspired every word of it.

Thank you, Brandon, for this particular year in the Team Hatmaker story. You have been a steady anchor through a stormy season. You deserve a prize for remaining fiercely true to your loud, impulsive, fiery bride. Someday I'm definitely going to turn precious, maybe.

I've never mentioned men here (am I sexist?), but I'd like to thank some good ones who stood strong with Brandon this year: Tray Pruet, David Daniels, David Smith, John Herrington, Andrew Barlow, Mark Groutas, Brent Phillips, Chad Zunker, Dad, Matt Carter, Andy Melvin, Hess Hester, Terry Fox, Brandon Thomas, Steve Murphy, Charlie Pennington, and The Denver Crew: Dennis Jeffreys, Alex Shootman, Mike Kilbane, Mike Nelson, and Scotty Priest. You will never understand how much I love you for believing in Brandon. You all have starring roles in "Adventures in Church Planting." (Sorry you won't get paid for it. It's low budget.)

If it sounds melodramatic to say that these girls saved my life this year, well, that's just par for the course with me. Special thanks to Mom, Lindsay, Trina, Steph, Laura, Christi, Molly, Stephanie, Anna, Michelle, Paige, and Jenny. You girls closed in like vultures when I needed you, and I mean that in a good way. I love you so much. Please stay my friends forever. I'll try to stop airing your dirty laundry in print.

How can I thank my editor, Karen Lee-Thorp, enough? You people cannot fathom how I ramble in print pre-editing. No one needs an editor worse than I do, and no editor is better than Karen. Thank you for sticking with me on this project. I'm totally codependent on you. No pressure.

To all my friends at NavPress: I don't know if it's an oversight on your part, but this is the sixth book of mine you've published. (What is *wrong* with y'all?) To beloved Kris Wallen, Dan Benson, Pamela Mendoza, Kathy Mosier (happy twins!), Darla Hightower, Arvid Wallen, Kathleen Campbell, Shelley Ring (bless you for the title concession), Jessica Chappell, Susan Riches, and Eric Grogg. Without you, I'm just a sarcastic girl with a laptop, wasting a lot of time. Thank you for believing in me. I'll try not to waste your money.

Finally, so much gratitude to my five girlfriends who let me tell their stories in the last chapter. Thank you for permission, and, more important, thanks for being the amazing, brave, obedient, compassionate women you are. You all get the gold star. Try to rub off on me more often.

Introduction

In the spirit of full disclosure, I thought I should crack open the unwashed window of my mind and reveal the warfare I've been fighting with myself over this book. Historically, I've been my own worst critic, and the mere idea of this subject has caused an internal civil war. The beautiful, fantastical, misunderstood subject of biblical womanhood is so essential, my fear of mishandling it nearly kept me sidelined.

Here are the mean thoughts in my head that point and laugh and cause me grief on par with the three boys who asked my cuter, more developed seventh-grade girlfriends why they were slumming with a dork like me at the county fair in 1986 and then proceeded to drape all over my friends (who had fortuitously sprouted booby buds) while hiding from me, which caused me to cry for an hour after collapsing on the lap of my mom, who thereby netted me some contacts to replace the bargain-selection nerd glasses that contributed to the trauma, because my mom is basically a bleeding heart who, after bawling with me, swore to run every one of them down with her station wagon in the junior high parking lot, which is exactly what I plan on doing the first time some ignorant boy makes the fatal decision to cross my angel daughter (we're not a gracious family). But back to the mean voices in my head:

- You're not old enough to write about this.
- You're not a good enough writer.

- You're hardly a model of superior femininity.
- Everyone else who addresses this subject is so much better than you.
- Everyone else who addresses this subject is so much more profound than you.
- Very definitely, you're going to screw this up somehow. Positively. Count on it.
- "Womanhood" is not a subject you're qualified for; try "How to Effectively Dodge Brownie Troop Leadership."

The mean voices have plenty to say about *you*, too:

- No one wants to read this.
- Everyone wants to read this, but only if Beth Moore writes it.
- Women will think you're trite, too irreverent, not eloquent, and probably special needs.
- The forty-seven women who might read this will compare it to a best seller, which we'll refrain from naming, and will find you rather urban with no appreciation for soft, flowing marital dialogue and blooming flowers.
- This book will tip women off, and they'll be on to you. You'll be exposed as the painfully regular, dysfunctional girl you are.

And every time enthusiasm raised its perky little head again, I'd do more research, meaning reading legitimate books on the same subject, then crawl back into my hole of insecurity and decide to write a funny book instead, because while other Christian writers *are* better than I am, they aren't a particularly funny bunch.

But that persistent God kept at it. Listen, if you don't know Him already, let me clue you in: He totally has an agenda, and He rarely takes no for an answer. A democracy our relationship is not. If you think you can ignore Him when you don't feel like doing something, I've got three words for you: The Holy Spirit. That guy can ruin your sleep patterns worse than a colicky baby. Oh, He pressed. This subject is seriously on His radar, and He has been whispering His thoughts on the matter until I simply couldn't *not* write this book. In fact, the ink hasn't dried on my contract (okay, I haven't even signed it yet), but I can't wait any longer. I must begin writing so I can start sleeping again.

So, girlfriends, I raise my voice with the wiser, more accomplished, and more experienced women who've gone before me. I join them in the worthy mission of reclaiming the utter loveliness of being a girl. While the Bible has been used to keep women subservient and silent, I believe that it is the textbook on femininity. Let's follow the surprising stories of the five women named in Jesus' lineage—Tamar, Rahab, Ruth, Bathsheba, and Mary—and expose some important myths and truths about what it means to be a woman. God is terribly passionate about His daughters. We are valuable, crucial, the highlight of the earth, and it's time we get that straight.

It's something of a slippery slope you've stepped onto, but you are so welcome here. Come with me, dear one, and let's get back in touch with our own favor. After all, we are women—beautiful, brilliant, beloved, blessed. God has declared it. The tidal waves of culture have raged against us since the garden, but a new day is dawning. Here comes the sun . . .

Wearing my shades,

Jen

CHAPTER 1

The Irrational Equation of Femininity

You Think I'm What?

I've never taken well to being stereotyped. It bothers me endlessly when someone tells me who to be or assumes they know who I am. You know the saying about *assume*, right? It makes a real pain in the butt out of you, or something like that. I suppose I feel that way because of who I am on paper. Here it is, in all its predictability: white, middle class, daughter of functional parents, minister's kid, honor student, Little Miss Churchy Churcherton, former teacher, pastor's wife, soccer mom, suburban dweller, Bible teacher, Starbucks enthusiast.

Yawn.

Because of my vanilla pedigree, I've always been drawn to rebellion. Now, mind you, my version of revolt is pretty small-time — a pseudo-rebellion, if you will. To counter the image as a high school cheerleader, I got into grunge. As the starting shortstop, I wore a ribbon in my ponytail. Do you see how controversial I was? As a card-carrying Christian, I tried cursing for a while, but it was like Al Gore attempting humor on *Letterman*: rather unconvincing. As a teacher, I played Guns N' Roses in my classroom, because that's the type of nonconformist I am.

Recently, dismayed at the cliché that I am, I got the top of my left ear pierced and spent the day positive that everyone was staring at my over-the-top street cred. I wear jeans instead of slacks. I wear cowboy boots when I should wear heels. And I don't want to shock you, but I'm graduating from the straight ticket voting sector. In fact, I recently said to a left-ish friend, "I suspect I'm getting liberal, but I'm not sure. Ask me some questions and help me decide." After a brief inquiry on issues like environmental awareness and social reform, she labeled me a "lazy, unmotivated moderate." I felt like I'd practically been jumped into a gang.

So this morning, as I hung up my cell phone while driving my SUV with leather captain's chairs and drop-down DVD player, my $4.37 mocha nestled in one of my thirty cup holders, I pondered how anti-establishment I am and thought about this book. (Roll eyes here.) The whole portrayal of a "godly woman" never set right with me. It's packaged as demure or matronly or subservient or highly precious, none of which I am and all of which ring hollow.

HATERS

A girl in her twenties recently told me how when she was a teen, her church shamed girls for their beauty, chastising them for destroying their brothers in Christ though they were poster girls for modesty. She was encouraged to skip college because it would conflict with her destiny as being "the lesser figure in her household." Eventually, she and her mother were asked to leave the church, because as a divorcée, her mother was too tainted. The girl nearly skipped her SATs and, big shock, has struggled with her identity in Christ ever since.

Lord in heaven, how can this still be going on? While hers is an extreme case, it illustrates a struggle that has raged since the garden. Women have been misunderstood, mistreated, and mischaracterized since creation deviated from perfection. We have struggled to find our place, to find our voice in what became a male-oriented world.

And let me say this: What you are reading is not a thinly veiled feminist book. I'm not trying to stick it to The Man. This is no battle cry for independence, because men are our beloved allies. We have equal standing at the gates of heaven, and together we are a force to be reckoned with. The confusion surrounding our identity does not rest only at the feet of men. There are many contributing factors to the feminine crisis, and that's what it is: a crisis.

What else can you call it when women have willingly given away their influence? When we've bolstered the objectification of our sisters? When we've huddled in passive silence doing everyone's bidding? When we bark and bite with a masculine swagger? While the Enemy claims our children, and men try to function without the tempering of our gifts, women slump on the sidelines, injured by guilt, frustration, and confusion. I see Christian women carrying a tension they can't alleviate: who they are versus who they think they should be. So they limp through life with the constant handicap of inadequacy.

BAD TIMES

Observe the moving target of womanhood in a secular sense. Culture has defined its daughters in many disturbing ways.

Although there's some evidence to suggest that it wasn't so bad to be a woman in prehistoric times before people settled down to be farmers, the patriarchal system in the ancient Mediterranean world embodied a sad, sorry descent of women's position. Women were devalued in their communities, in their families, in the minds of men. They were voiceless; men's natural aggression ran unchecked and was used against women rather than for them as God intended. Our sisters were possessions, a small notch above slaves.

Ancient Mesopotamia forced some women into ritual prostitution as part of their worship. The warrior Greek culture treated women as booty and property, and the later Greeks were downright contemptuous of women. They didn't educate them; the Athenians kept them locked away from the public; philosophers suggested that men take male lovers for intelligent communication while keeping women simply for childbearing.

The philosopher Plato wrote, "All those creatures generated as men who proved themselves cowardly and spent their lives in wrongdoing were transformed, at their second incarnation, into women."

Aristotle added, "The female is a monstrosity, a deformed male; a deformity which occurs in the ordinary course of nature."

The great Athenian orator Demosthenes commented, "Mistresses we keep for the sake of pleasure, concubines for the daily care of our persons, but wives to bear us legitimate children."[1]

And as my editor, Karen, said, "Don't even get me started on the Romans." Let's just say that Roman law allowed men to kill their wives for drunkenness (which would lead them to adultery, obviously) and forced families to raise all male babies unless crippled, while every baby girl could be disposed of unless she was firstborn. This was evidenced by burial records showing twice as many male adult burials as females.[2]

Obviously, I'm painting with a wide brush, and certainly there were loved women and daughters during those centuries. But the general rule was "Men first, women a very distant second." It was unquestioned, and we see its imprint in God's Word as it chronicles the flavor of those times. But be certain, dear girls, that recorded history in God's Word doesn't mean He approved. The Bible bears witness to the sin of mankind from the first page. And while other cultures suffocated the spirit of their women, God's Word holds countless examples of the favor He reserved for them. But we'll get there.

It's a sad commentary that the reduction of women lasted so long, lasts still in much of the world. When I hear of some of our Islamic sisters being beaten into submission and of the genital mutilation performed on the five-year-old girls of some African groups, my heart cries out for holy intervention. The baby girls of China are thrown out like garbage, and Vietnamese families are selling their daughters into sex trafficking for $150 or less. It's tragically reported:

> The enslaved girls must stay until their debt to their purchasers is paid off, or face beatings. This is difficult, if not impossible, since the owners consider the girls indebted to them for their constantly mounting expenses for food, clothing, medical costs and abortions. As a result, a brothel owner will hold a girl prisoner until she becomes too old or too ill to attract customers.[3]

Father, help us.

> The LORD works righteousness
>   and justice for *all* the oppressed. (Psalm 103:6, emphasis
>   added)

The ramifications of this promise are boundless. Can we fathom how God deals with oppressed women raised in pagan faith systems? How does He judge the poisonous, hurtful woman abused as a girl? What will be eternally decided for the self-destructive daughter of the streets? If the Lord works not only justice but also righteousness for the oppressed, grace will burrow much deeper than we hoped.

Someday we'll stand as the daughters of Eve, clothed in white, redeemed by our Savior, rescued from exploitation, violence, and centuries of dishonor.

"God is amazing," wrote Lisa Bevere in *Fight Like a Girl*, "for even now He is taking the sword of His Word and turning things around for His daughters. The very sword that has been at times used against us will soon battle on our behalf. He is carrying out His decree of everlasting love and restoring the correct order and position of honor for His sons and daughters."[4] God is not silent. The assault against women has not gone unnoticed. His intervention on behalf of His daughters is legendary. Yet a day is coming when vengeance will be entirely His.

Take heart, sisters. Restoration awaits.

BURNED LAMB BONES

However, because women in the last century were anxious to speed up this process, the pendulum swung too far. A hopeful feminine awakening took a downward turn. And I get it. I get good ideas that tanked, since that is basically my life mantra.

For example, one semester in my small, living-room Bible study, my girlfriends and I studied Luke. We read about Jesus' crucifixion on Passover and evaluated every symbolic detail of that Jewish holiday. Well, with enthusiastic good intentions, I secretly arranged a Passover meal, scripted readings and all. I cannot tell you how pleased with myself I was. I felt so Jesus-y shopping in the kosher section for matzo ball recipes.

For a Passover meal, one element of the seder plate is a lamb shank bone. My online Jewish muses suggested I ask my butcher for a clean lamb bone, and it might even be free. Thank you very much, but it was $2.13, a figure I remember because I paid it twice, but I'm getting ahead of myself.

Evidently, you boiled the bone until it was clean, white, and presentable for the seder plate. I guess decomposing flesh rotting on the Passover table wasn't exactly WJWD. So the morning before, I put my lamb bone on the stove and realized it was time to take Caleb to preschool. Because it was only five minutes away, I decided to leave the lamb a-boiling.

But as I seem to have a short-term memory problem, when my Girlfriend Trina called en route begging me to come over for coffee, I said what any responsible, aware girl would say: "Lord, yes! If I stay home, I'll have to do laundry." And straight from preschool I drove, not to my house with the boiling baby sheep bone, but to hers.

As you can imagine, this story does not end well.

After sipping java for, count 'em, two hours, Trina asked the fateful question: "How's your big surprise Passover going?" And I got that feeling. That bad gut check when you know something is terribly wrong but it's fuzzy. Then, tragically, I knew. I flew out her door, my dad's words from the high school years echoing in the vacuous space between my ears: "Jennifer, for a 4.0 student, sometimes you're dumb as a board."

Clearly, he had a point.

When I threw open my front door, so much black smoke billowed out, I couldn't see, because apparently water will eventually boil out, leaving lamb skeleton and fire. I took a deep breath, ran to the kitchen, opened the back door, and threw out the charred pot. I opened every window, every door, and unplugged every smoke alarm. Three days and five bottles of Febreze later, the house still smelled like death with a hint of floral.

My girlfriends' husbands, who fancy themselves funny types, left messages on my cell phone: "Tell me, Clarice, when will the lambs stop screaming?" Oh, that's cute. Let's all laugh at the Bible teacher who lied during Lamb Bone Purchase Number Two by telling the butcher I was having two seder plates, that's all. And who was he? The Passover police? What did I look like? An idiot who burned the baby lamb bones symbolic of her Christian Lord and Savior?

WHAT DID THAT STORY HAVE TO DO WITH ANYTHING, YOU ASK?

Anyway, my point is, sometimes an honorable nugget of an idea goes bad. That's what I think happened to the feminist movement, when women decided they had a glory to recover. This is pure conjecture, but I wonder if the seeds of change weren't initially planted by God. Before you gasp, declaring feminism a purely secular attack on family and womanhood, consider it. *Could* God have stirred up passion for the power of the feminine? *Might* He have begun unveiling the glory He intended for His daughters only to have it jerked from His hands and turned into a self-serving movement?

It wouldn't be the first time God enacted change only to have it polluted by mankind. The church was barely five seconds old when its congregants spread Gnosticism and other false teachings. And no sooner had the Holy Spirit inhabited believers than they misused the gifts He administered. Then the evangelistic commission was turned into a blunt instrument, widening the gap between the lost and found. These were all God's ideas, but as we'd stipulate, people have a knack for making a mess of things.

Yet God has this, well, godly way of turning even the largest wayward ships around. The speed with which He commandeered this voyage of feminism is what makes me consider its origins. We're less than a century from the time women first received the right to vote, half a century from more radical assertions of equality, and already women are rising up to participate with God in separating the wheat from the chaff. While male domination lasted for millennia, this new breach of gender conduct is already being soothed.

Could it be because this one had roots in the heavens and the other was birthed from rebellion? Perhaps what God began He can more quickly reclaim.

Not unlike the Babylonian captivity that Israel endured for seventy years. How many Hebrews believed *that* was God's doing? Surely they thought He'd abandoned them. They were oppressed, mistreated, strangers to their former glory. Yet God has a history of using short-term captivity to bring forth lasting change, captivity He not only allowed but commissioned. God can initiate a season—activated by sin—that appears worse than before. But as quickly as it started, He ends it. As God said of Israel's restoration,

> Surely, as I have planned, so it will be,
>   and as I have purposed, so it will stand. . . .
> [The] yoke will be taken from my people,
>   and his burden removed from their shoulders.
> This is the plan determined for the whole world;
>   this is the hand stretched out over all nations.
> For the LORD Almighty has purposed, and who can
>   thwart him? (Isaiah 14:24-27)

Could centuries of sins against women prompt God to birth feminism, harsh and misguided as it briefly was, only to recover the reins and execute justice? Rebellious sin (men against women), temporary captivity (feministic chaos), righteousness—it is indeed His pattern. Couldn't we define feminism as temporary captivity? While many women recoil at that, hindsight reveals women trapped between their hearts and the "new image" they were supposed to project. Men and children were caught in the carnage, left to fend for themselves. While women screamed and swore, the nation was tangled in a battle of the sexes.

Women were no longer defined by men but by each other. Men were the enemy, and war was waged. Women were told to be aggressive, loud, definitely furious. The differences between genders were dismissed as irrelevant—no, nonexistent. "The cramped little categories of personality and social function to which we assign people from birth must be broken open so that all people can develop independently, as individuals," wrote Jo Freeman, editor of the *Voice of the Women's Liberation Movement* in 1971. "This means that there will be an integration of social functions and life styles of men and women as a group until, ideally, one cannot tell anything of relevance about a person's social role by knowing their sex. . . . No longer will humanity suffer a schizophrenic personality desperately trying to reconcile its 'masculine' and 'feminine' parts."[5]

Say what? Love to the women's libbers, but did they ever actually meet a man? One glance at little boys playing death-by-army-troopers while girls played house and wedding day was some indicator of design. An integration of social functions? Ladies, hands up if your man is remotely capable of doing half the things you do. And I don't mean laundry and carpool; I'm talking about being the glue that holds your family together. And let me tell you something: If my gender tells you nothing about my identity, then go ahead and introduce my husband to a mistress and sign my kids up for therapy. If "wife" and "mom" have no discernable standing in my life, then I'm just an angry chick who'd sacrifice her family for a selfish movement.

Oh, wait. That *is* what happened.

But I did wonder if God started this thing, didn't I? See, the thing is, there were a few crazy years when women abandoned their posts. But is my little eye the only one that spies the wheat that separated from the chaff? In progressive cultures, I see women valued for their backbreaking efforts again. I see pages of legislation enacted on behalf of women. I see moms who transitioned from the isolation of their homes into a sisterhood of togetherness. I see women standing up for the abused, the poor, the lost members of their feminine tribe. I see women rising up on behalf of the globally oppressed. I see an unprecedented support network for all facets of womanhood. Our issues are no longer taboo. We have the freedom to speak up, speak out, ask for help, lean on our sisters.

All that smacks of God.

Even as we speak, the radical extremes of the feminist movement are receding. I observe this with a modicum of detachment, because I was too young to march on the front lines. The battle was diminishing by the time I could comprehend it. On behalf of my generation, I believe we're pursuing center. We have the benefit of retrospection on the two extremes of the last millennium, neither healthy. We recognize the oppression of being subservient male accessories as well as the danger of turning into contentious, genderless semi-females.

"BE QUIET" – LOVE, THE CHURCH

How did the church keep up with the trends? Not too well, I'm afraid. Or perfectly well, if you look at it from that angle. The one place women should've found relief from male domination perpetuated it. "You will immediately recognize women who are dominated," wrote Lisa Bevere. "To our shame, far too often their ranks overflow in the church. After so many years of intimate mistreatment, they seem to shrink within themselves. You can actually sense their husbands' disapproval or rejection in their physical demeanor."[6]

Imagine me crying a river knowing the weapon of coercion was God's Holy Word, my very favorite thing. Scripture was taken out of context and wielded as a bludgeoning tool. As simple as it sounds to cast blame on the fellas, most were simply behaving according to current gender models (as were the women, I'll remind you). It was what it was, and no one questioned it. Scripture was interpreted in such a way, and all the players acted appropriately. That's the saddest commentary: Both sides really believed their limited roles. Women's silence was their loveliest offering—plus their obvious nursery and dining hall duties.

The church is jogging toward change, albeit slowly. I was recently asked to deliver the Sunday message at a very large traditional Baptist church in Houston. "Nervous" is a light treatment of my anxiety level. Think thousands of people, men in suits. During the prelude, I sat with the pastor's aide assigned to babysitting me. With shaking hands, I looked through my notes while talking myself out of pro-jectile vomiting. The assistant leaned over, ever so nonchalantly, and offered up this little nugget: "You know, in all our history, we've had a woman deliver the Sunday message only once. The funny thing is, a bunch of people walked out."

Oh, that's real funny, you girl with the talking mouth who clearly has a discernment problem. I stared blankly at her, wondering if sheer will could undo the carnage she had casually unleashed into my psyche. I believe she will be punished for that comment someday, which brings me great pleasure, but merciful heavens! It's a wonder I walked up to their forty-foot platform and uttered one solitary word. Sources tell me it was mostly intelligible, though all I remember was waving my arms and smiling too much and one questionable com-ment on plastic surgery. (And no one walked out, thank Jesus.)

Perhaps the tides are turning even under the steeples. Not that I believe women should hijack every pulpit, but we are smarter and more educated, anointed, and biblically proficient than ever. Female scholars, apologists, theologians, writers, teachers, speakers, minis-ters, leaders, activists, visionaries—they exist in droves and are work-ing beautifully with men to present the most balanced, unbiased discussion on Scripture ever available. I've heard teaching from women that has altered the trajectory of my life. Women have much to offer the church beyond traditional service.

More about that in chapter 3 on Smart Girls.

"YOU'VE GOT GAME" — LOVE, GOD

So it seems men, culture, other women, religious models, the church, and various movements have taken turns telling women who to be. The human static of anger, domination, inferiority, aggression, fear, and ego has made a clear interpretation impossible. But it occurs to me to ask a different question — or better yet, a different source:

God, who do *You* say we are?

Even as I write that, I'm flooded with relief. I've never been certain of my standing with men (Do they find me obnoxious? Loud? Book-smart, not street-smart?) or with women (I was once evaluated by a conference attendee as being "a little harsh"). I've never exactly matched a cultural or religious model of femininity. My position as a Bible teacher is met with applause by some enthusiasts, while one man stomped off upon hearing I was filling in for my pastor. So the church verdict is still out. And even some female leaders I admire offer a definition of femininity that wears like a big-sister's dress. I'd have to undergo a lobotomy to fit into it.

But there is another voice above the din of humanity:

Bring my sons from afar
    and my daughters from the ends of the earth —
everyone who is called by my name,
    whom I created for my glory,
    whom I formed and made. (Isaiah 43:6-7)

Our design was invented in the heavens, sisters. We are uniquely formed for God's glory. We are deliberate and beautiful, diverse and powerful, sealed by the name of the Most High. He took great care to create us, every detail and facet. In Him our identity is settled. We are daughters of the King—valued, adored, crucial. Anyone else's take on us is irrelevant.

> This is what the LORD says—
> > he who created you, O Jacob,
> > he who formed you, O Israel:
> "Fear not, for I have redeemed you;
> > I have summoned you by name; you are mine."
> > (Isaiah 43:1)

There is a superior opinion of us that exists.

With what can only be described as reverent holy fear, my aim is to open Scripture and discover what God thinks about His daughters. Who are we? What are we supposed to do? To be? What about when we add men to the equation? Are we secondary humans? When You look at us, You're thinking what? How should we cope with the assault on femininity? What's our responsibility for our international sisters? What pleases You about us? What value do we hold? What's so great about being a girl?

As you can see, the mental warfare I referenced has some merit. These are questions rooted in the ages. But as God eloquently put it, we've been summoned. It is time to rise up, girls. The call has been issued. I believe there is a holiness awaiting our generation. *We are the ones.* If we abdicate this responsibility, I shudder to think what lies ahead for our sisters behind us and abroad who are counting on our intervention. Yet there is a glimmer on the horizon of possibility if we don the righteous glory of womanhood and claim our redemption. It is ours to recover.

Let the daughters return from the ends of the earth.

Shake off your dust;
    rise up, sit enthroned, O Jerusalem.
Free yourself from the chains on your neck,
    O captive Daughter of Zion. (Isaiah 52:2)

CHAPTER 2

Greater Than, Less Than, or Equal

Doormats, Cavemen, and Other Dumb Ideas

Myth #1:

Women are defined by the men in their lives.

Genesis 38

The following kernels were found in seven seconds with my trusty laptop:

- How many chauvinists does it take to change a lightbulb? None. The chick can wash in the dark!
- Why do men die before their wives? They want to.
- Women! Can't live with 'em, pass the beer nuts!
- In the beginning, God created the earth and rested. Then God created Man and rested. Then God created Woman. Since

then, neither God nor Man has rested.

- What's worse than a male chauvinist pig? A woman who won't do what she's told.
- How do you know when a woman is about to say something smart? When she starts her sentence with, "A man once told me . . ."
- Scientists have discovered a food that diminishes a woman's sex drive by 90 percent: wedding cake.
- Women will never be equal to men until they can walk down the street with a bald head and a beer gut and still think they're sexy.

Okay, that last one is a little funny, but do you cringe like me when you read these? Feel that bizarre tension between your head and heart? Our heads understand this as foolish drivel we should print out and line our litter boxes with, but our hearts often whisper a different story. Our hearts confirm that yes, this *is* how we are perceived. This *is* how men talk about us. We are a thorn. We are unmanageable. We are needed only for function. As crystallized in *Captivating*, "You're too much, and not enough."[1] Women are a problem.

Doesn't that resonate with your history? Our incessant talking, our relentless pressure to evaluate, our whining, nagging, neediness—these threaten to overwhelm our feminine dignity. I'm torn between being wrongfully typecast and becoming disgusted with my own gender. I sense a brilliant plan by our Enemy, because of two possible responses: I will despise either men for disrespecting us or women for deserving it.

The whole affair undermines the intentionality of our design. Let there be no doubt: "He created them male and female and blessed them. And when they were created, he called them 'man'" (Genesis 5:2). Unique from each other yet set together, we are mankind. We are gifted differently, but our power is in our union. We got hung up on the first part ("He created them male and female") and forgot the second ("and blessed them").

Case in point: Maybe these sound more familiar (but, I add, they were harder to find):

- I married beneath me. All women do.
- Women have their faults, but men only have two: everything they say and everything they do.
- Why do men like smart women? Opposites attract.
- How many men does it take to screw in a lightbulb? One—he just holds it up there and waits for the world to revolve around him.
- What do you call a man with half a brain? Gifted.
- Why are all dumb-blonde jokes one-liners? So men can understand them.
- How is Colonel Sanders like the typical male? All he's concerned with is legs, breasts, and thighs.

It's so easy. It takes no courage to say, "Men are brutes"; "Sex, food, and sports are the holy trinity"; "They are as sensitive as fertilizer"; and so on. With a dismissive wave, we write the whole thing off by turning the superiority game on its end. Yet if ever an eye for an eye fell short, it is in the disrespect between the sexes. Fighting back is for those who lack vision. It is the uncreative response to gender inequality.

WHERE WAS ADAM AT EVE'S CREATION? ASLEEP.

Before I discuss a better way, we must acknowledge how these stereotypes shaped us. After we set aside the feministic noise, the independent façade, and the pretense of confidence, legions of women remain poorly defined by the men in their lives. Christian women everywhere bear the wounds of dishonor: neglect, abuse, abandonment, hatred, rape, betrayal, disrespect. I don't know which stripes you've endured, if any, but the results are the same: fear, insecurity, anger, bitterness, distrust, paranoia, fury. Do you see your reflection?

What do we do? "Our definition or image of being female should not be passed again through the parameters of man," wrote Lisa Bevere. "Adam was not involved in Eve's creation; he was asleep."[2] We have a whole purposeful identity outside of men, perhaps in spite of men. It is messy work, but we must reclaim it—not to enforce our separateness, but to take that restored identity and insert it back into our relationships with our fathers, exes, husbands, sons. Together, God called us man. Women aren't to be a tribe unto ourselves, but our identity can be recovered from men who've falsely defined us.

How does God intersect our history? How does He feel about the injuries His daughters endured by His sons? Is even He capable of restoring women after such oppression? Let's find relief from the Word. It is chock-full of losers, screwups, victims, and unlikely heroes, thank goodness. It was a ragtag bunch with a myriad of dysfunctions. There isn't a situation we've endured that isn't echoed in Scripture.

ONCE UPON A HOLY KINGDOM . . .

We'll spend these next two chapters discussing a woman whose story might seem painfully familiar (and a bit outrageous and weird). By the way, have you noticed that certain Bible stories are flat bizarre? The Sunday school board decidedly left some out of their approved curriculum, because I was a grown-up (a loose term) when I stumbled onto the story of Tamar and Judah.

If you'd like to read along, go back to the beginning in Genesis 38. Here we get this story of righteousness (eventually), with some highly embarrassing beginnings. Before we go on, take a deep breath and feel relieved by that. Embarrassing beginnings, anyone? As we say in Texas, you're fixin' to feel better about yourself.

It's before the nation of Israel—no temple, no priests, no Law, no prophets yet. It's just one man called forward to start the whole thing. Abraham (finally) had Isaac, Isaac had Jacob, and Jacob had twelve sons, whom the tribes of Israel were later named after. One of them, Joseph, who had something of a discernment problem, was hated by his brothers for being Daddy's favorite and broadcasting these pesky dreams of superiority he kept having. So the other eleven sold him into slavery, dipped his robe into goat's blood, and told Daddy he'd been ravaged by a wild animal.

A lovely commencement for the twelve tribes of Israel.

That's not the only embarrassing beginning. It was just after this escapade that Judah, Jacob's fourth-oldest son, left the Promised Land to seek a new fortune among the pagan Canaanites. This is the same Judah who brought Joseph's shredded robe to his father and said, "We found this. Examine it to see whether it is your son's robe." Are you getting the Judah picture? He was a member of the only protected family on earth, yet his jealousies and greed removed him from the family blessings before he hit his twenties.

Big shock, Judah married a Canaanite's daughter and she became pregnant. This was forbidden under the covenant that God established with Abraham. So this guy is racking up strikes like some kind of preacher's kid. Judah and his wife had three sons. It's easy to miss the gap, but Genesis 38:5 ends with the birth of son number three, and verse 6 says, "Judah got a wife for Er, his firstborn, and her name was Tamar." Before we meet Tamar, let's acknowledge the entire generation that Judah lived with godless people. He spent years removed from the holiness of God. His family had no opportunity to raise him in the Lord. Idol worship? Probably. Judah has completely forfeited his identity by the time we meet Tamar.

BAD BOYS, BAD BOYS, WHATCHA GONNA DO?

Girls, as you look at the men historically in your life—dad, brothers, boyfriends, caregivers, other family members, neighbors, husbands, even sons—it might help to take a critical look at the identities they forfeited too. However some man's existence shaped you, remember he was shaped first. If a man wounded you in any way, it might bring relief to acknowledge his history.

Perhaps he was mistreated, injured, or poorly loved by his dad, like Judah. Maybe his family was a freak show of dysfunction. Did he develop nasty habits simply to survive his circumstances? Maybe he learned unhealthy patterns so young, he couldn't break them. Perhaps he never had one godly person to show him how. Abandoned boys sometimes grow into men who abandon. Boys who were beaten can turn into men who don't know another way. If you see that man as a six-year-old boy, can you find some compassion? Can you feel his pain, or at least understand the course of his life?

On the other hand, some people are born with an evil bent. They've suffocated any remnant of God's image. Their instincts drift to violence and hatred for humanity. Paul wrote of people like this: "They are darkened in their understanding and separated from the life of God because of the ignorance that is in them due to the hardening of their hearts. Having lost all sensitivity, they have given themselves over to sensuality so as to indulge in every kind of impurity, with a continual lust for more" (Ephesians 4:18-19). They are insatiable vessels of destruction, poisoned from the inside out.

I bring up both scenarios not to excuse their behavior but to offer this: Whether the man who hurt you falls into the first or second category, it wasn't your fault. You did not deserve mistreatment, nor were you the cause of it. Can you see that? Some men lash out or leave because of chronic internal pain. Other men behave that way from the evil in their hearts. Regardless, their true identities were forfeited, and you got caught in the fallout.

There is a comfort in embracing your innocence. I'm not overlooking your contributions to a toxic relationship, but in every encounter between a wayward man and his target, there is a degree of innocence. No woman deserves to be hit. No woman should be verbally assaulted. No woman deserves to be abandoned or neglected. And she is never the source of a man's mistreatment, no matter what he says. A righteous man does not circumstantially abuse. And God's position is clear:

> Arise, LORD! Lift up your hand, O God.
>> Do not forget the helpless.
> Why does the wicked man revile God?
>> Why does he say to himself, "He won't call me to
>> account"?
> But you, O God, do see trouble and grief;
>> you consider it to take it in hand.
> *The victim commits himself to you*;
>> you are the helper of the fatherless.
> Break the arm of the wicked and evil man;
>> call him to account for his wickedness
>> that would not be found out.
>
> The LORD is King for ever and ever;
>> the nations will perish from his land.
> You hear, O LORD, the desire of the afflicted;
>> you encourage them, and you listen to their cry,
> defending the fatherless and the oppressed,
>> *in order that man, who is of the earth, may terrify no more.*
>> (Psalm 10:12-18, emphasis added)

This world is not fair, dear one, but God is. If you suffered in silence and justice never came, don't imagine that God didn't see it. He will take it in His hand, and I wouldn't want to be on the wrong side of that hand. You are defended by almighty God. Believe your innocence. Ask the Lord to separate your identity from the lies you absorbed from a carnal man. Allow his history to saturate your knowledge, and allow that knowledge to permeate the darkness.

You did not create the sin in his heart. You were not responsible for the early pain he endured. You did not cause him to forfeit his true identity. Nothing you could've done or stopped doing would have fixed what was broken inside him. You maybe reaped the repercussions, but you didn't cause the breach.

Receive that.

WHY JUDAH AND COMPANY BOTHER ME

As we encounter the next collection of bad choices in Tamar's story, I'm reminded how aggravating it is to deal with someone who refuses to play by the rules. Case in point: Like all moms, the amount of time I spend in the car with my kids is grounds for homicide or substance abuse. Before I embraced my inner genius and installed a DVD player, we played car games so I wouldn't arrive at my destinations with bulging neck veins and crying children.

My oldest two, seven and five then, laid out the rules of each game. For their personality types, rules are not a gray area. There is the right way to play, then the cheater's way, which brings me to the youngest contestant in the car. Caleb, at three, brought a unique level of individualism to each game. The regulations were more like suggestions for him.

For example, "I Spy" has always been a car staple. If grass was the secret object in play, the oldest two said something like, "I spy something green and soft and low to the ground." I'm not Mensa material, but I typically followed their clues to the correct object. Caleb, on the other hand, would say, "I spy something. It's the green grass," so the element of mystery was fairly lost.

Or take for instance "Animal Quiz," another Hatmaker favorite. One person would silently choose an animal, and we asked questions until we figured out what it was. The dialogue with the rule followers would go something like:

Where does it live?	The desert.
How many legs does it have?	Four.
Does it have scales or fur?	Scales.
What does it eat?	Bugs.
Is it a lizard?	Yes!

But with Caleb, it went more like (and this is verbatim):

Where does it live?	Somewhere in the world.
How many legs does it have?	Forty.
Does it have scales or fur?	Yes.
What does it eat?	Cereal.
(Silence on our part.)	It's a clam.

The unhappy duet would wail, "Moooommmmm!!" While trying not to laugh, I explained (again) why we let Caleb play our games even though he was unconcerned with the actual rules. Frankly, I enjoy his liberties—otherwise, I'm decoding "I spy something white and fluffy up in the sky" all the time, which makes me soft in the brain after a while. But his fellow contestants have zero tolerance, because to them it's not fair.

Tamar was in a family of men who refused to play by the rules, and it was definitely unfair. She married Er, but "Er, Judah's first-born, was wicked in the LORD's sight; so the Lord put him to death." Let's think about this. Why did Er have to play by God's rules? He never met his grandfather Jacob or his great-grandfather Isaac. In fact, he knew nobody on that side of the family. His mom, aunts, uncles, grandparents, extended family—all Canaanites. He didn't sign the covenant with God, yet his wickedness ended his short life.

Girls, God held Er accountable because of Judah's responsibility to God. There was one chosen man in that family, but God included the whole troop in the plan. Hear this:

Men are held to a high standard for their family's sake.

God made a promise to Judah's great-grandfather Abraham, and He wasn't going back. He was fulfilling His vow to make a great nation out of Abraham's descendants, granting him as many offspring as stars in the sky. So if Judah foolishly decided to marry into the Canaanite culture, well, it wasn't God's problem. Judah was a name bearer for the family—a descendant maker, if you will. God had a nation to build, and He wouldn't suffer any wickedness.

It should encourage us that God requires spiritual integrity of men for the sake of the family. If God lowered the bar, how many wives and children would be ruined from a lax policy? What if God ignored Er's depravity? One guess who would suffer most: Tamar, and every child she would've borne for him.

Er's evil ended his chance to be an ancestor of Jesus, yet God kept Tamar in the story. This mixed-faith family was a questionable cast, but God works with what He has. He evaluated Er and Tamar, and only she was worthy of His namesake, though Er had Abraham's blood in his veins.

God weighed Tamar's value separately from Er's. He wouldn't saddle her with a wicked man, even if he could put some stars in the sky for Abraham. So as we move forward, you will hate how she is victimized, but remember: God protected her and showed her favor from the beginning.

LOSER #2

This sounds bizarre, but after Er died, Judah instructed his next son, Onan, to marry Tamar and produce children in his dead brother's name. This was one of God's rules then, albeit a strange one. A "levirate marriage" was when a man died leaving his wife childless and his brother would take one for the team and give her babies. Those children would take the name of the dead husband and, thus, continue the family line.

Onan the rule breaker didn't want to follow this one, because if Tamar remained childless, *his* kids would receive the firstborn inheritance, a big deal then. Get this: Scripture tells us that "whenever he lay with his brother's wife, he spilled his semen on the ground to keep from producing offspring for his brother." No use standing on principle, right? He didn't want to get her pregnant, but couldn't he still have some fun? Don't get me started.

Bless her. We don't know what wickedness she suffered from Er, but she certainly did. Then the next loser in the family takes sexual advantage of her while not alleviating the devastation of being childless. Onan kicked her while she was down. You feeling her?

Certain men have radar for vulnerable women. They take advantage of their pain, maybe their desperation. My heart breaks when I see women like this. Hope gives way to despair, their identity reduced to a fraction of their worth. One too many injuries have taken their toll. These women slump from one unhealthy relationship to another, repeating patterns, losing themselves along the way. They finally shrink away. They never break the cycle and they wait for the grave, certain that ruin at the hands of men is all they can expect. But don't overlook this: "What [Onan] did was wicked in the LORD's sight; so he put him to death also."

"There is an amazing combination found when you marry strength with beauty, authority with wisdom, male with female," wrote Lisa Bevere. "It was always God's idea . . . two with one heart. The man's strength was never meant to be used against woman, but for her. Superior strength was given to men to protect and provide for the women in their lives. This strength was never meant to be an instrument of domination or abuse. Weak, confused, powerless men abuse women."[3]

Girls, take heart. God cares how His sons treat His daughters. If they are wicked, there will be a reckoning—not only for the kingdom but also for every woman and child valued in the heavens. Men may abuse their position, but God was dead serious when He commanded, "Love your wives, just as Christ loved the church and gave himself up for her" (Ephesians 5:25).

As a woman, you are precious and worthy, important and necessary. You hold value within your relationships, and, more important, you were credited with value the moment you were born. That basic human value transformed into a stunning holiness when you took the name of Christ. Before you were a daughter, sister, wife, mother, you were a delight to God, who designed your every facet and sent you to earth, a gift to all who would know you.

GLORY GIRLS

You created my inmost being . . .
My frame was not hidden from you
      when I was made in the secret place.
When I was woven together in the depths of the
      earth,

your eyes saw my unformed body.

All the days ordained for me

were written in your book

before one of them came to be. (Psalm 139:13,15-16)

God knit together your humor, beauty, talents, charm. The Holy Spirit decided which gifts to crown you with. Jesus took one look at the plan of you and declared, "I would have still died on that cross if only for this one."

Sisters, I believe that women are the apple of God's eye. It is common knowledge that daddies have a soft spot for their daughters. Jacqueline Jakes calls us "God's trophy women," contrasted to the shallow concept of "trophy wives":

> Basically, these women are like pieces of jewelry: they are accessories to the men. . . . While trophy wives are little more than pleasure seekers who are happy just to shine on their husbands' shelves, God's Trophy Women are far more valuable than decorations. They have become rich in spirit and taken on a value "worth far more than rubies" (Proverbs 31:10). They have engaged in battle and won. As a result, these women are trophies in God's curio, treasured possessions of the Most High God.[4]

Lord have mercy, yes! How I adore the men in some of your lives who affirmed your blessedness. The dad who will go to the grave swearing you were the daughter of his dreams, the husband who would take a bullet for the bride he can't believe he snagged. For the men who looked with spiritual eyes and saw the treasure of you, amen and amen. If you've even had one man who confirmed your value, then you've seen a glimpse of God's intentions. That's what He wanted all along.

But if that scenario is foreign, know this: You are still celebrated in the heavens, no matter what any man has said or done to the contrary. There is more to you than what any human concludes, good or bad. When it comes to your worth, Jesus had the final say when He prayed, "I have given them the glory that you gave me" (John 17:22). No one can take away your glory that Jesus paid for through His death and resurrection.

No one.

Your glory is not conditional on a perfect childhood or stellar father. It cannot be shaken by abuse or abandonment. It isn't disqualified by anyone's opinion. Even your own shortfalls cannot usurp the glory that is yours. God will never change His mind about your position as His glory bearer.

The only way to forfeit your glory is to give it away yourself. When we believe lies and continually play the victim, refusing to walk like a beloved daughter, our glory drains out like the finest wine out of a cracked goblet. Even when God uses His Spirit and teachers and fellow workers to pour our glory back in, the broken vessel can't hold it.

I wish there were some formula to get you there, but it comes down to this: You can either believe God's opinion of you or not. Read His words and say either yes or no. If you'll begin to say yes — even if you don't believe it yet — He'll win you over.

If that seems too simplistic, let me ask you this: Have you *ever* said yes to your own blessedness? Have you *ever* chosen God's opinion over man's? If not, then you actually have no idea the healing that awaits you. God urges us to "believe" and "trust" Him 237 times in His Word. Imagine what would happen if we believed Him when He said,

- "I take delight in my people." (Isaiah 65:19)
- "You are the work of my hands; I'm showing off through you." (Isaiah 60:21)

- "I've put a tiara of honor on your head." (Psalm 8:5)
- "You are my finest craftsmanship." (Ephesians 2:10)
- "You are my daughter." (2 Corinthians 6:18)
- "I have chosen you, and my Son prays for you when you feel condemned." (Romans 8:33-34)

There is power in our belief. God only told us that ten thousand times. Or look at it this way: Believing Him is all you *can* do. You can't erase your history or change someone's mind. You can't forget what's been said or done. You can't will yourself to health. You can only believe that what God says about you is true, let His strength inhabit that belief, and allow that strength to work its magic.

He can restore your glory if you let Him.

MORE HATERS

One last segment of Tamar's story for now: Er was wicked and put to death. Onan dishonored Tamar and was put to death. At that point, Judah freaked out. For his money, Tamar was a husband killer, a bad-luck chick. What? The mess he and his sons created, you say? Well, Judah needed a scapegoat, and Tamar fit the bill. He overlooked his and his sons' spiritual abdication and identified Tamar as the problem.

Land o' living. Have you ever been wrongly blamed by a man who wouldn't own his poor choices? This is the plight of the abused woman, the unwanted daughter, the girl whose date wouldn't accept no. *She deserved it. She pushed me too far. Her mother forced this pregnancy; I never wanted a kid. Her body language said yes. She was dressed like she wanted it.*

This pattern has been around since Genesis. The stronger blames the weaker; the bully blames the victim; the rich blame the poor. If you've been on the low end of this deal, be so vindicated by Jesus. He always took the underdog's side, saying stuff like:

- The last will be first, and the first will be last.
- Whoever humbles himself like this child is the greatest in my world.
- Do not look down on one of these little ones.
- My blessings are for the poor in spirit, the mourning, the meek, the persecuted.
- Leave her alone. (I love that one.)
- I came to bring good news, freedom, recovery, and favor for the marginalized.

When power is abused at the expense of the vulnerable, Jesus goes crazy. If the high fault the low, they better duck. Nothing made Jesus more furious. He has an affinity for the hurting and zero tolerance for those who took advantage.

It's almost a terrifying position to protect another, to guard her vulnerability and secure her honor, because Jesus is like her overzealous caseworker. He's watching, boy. He had no qualms telling those types that if they misused their strength *against* rather than *for*, they should save Him the trouble, tie a boulder around their necks, and jump into the lake. In fact, Jesus said "it would be better" than His vengeance (see Matthew 18:5-7). (If your image of Jesus involves Him loving the kittens and petting the lambs, you've obviously never read the Gospels.)

SAD TIMES

Which brings me to the saddest part: Judah told Tamar to "live as a widow in your father's house until my [youngest] son Shelah grows up," but he had no intention to let them marry, "for he thought, 'He may die too, just like his brothers.'" Rather than treat her respectfully, Judah sent her away with her broken life. Out of sight, out of mind. Good riddance to the bad-luck charm.

There she stayed for "a long time." Horror.

Her youth wasted away as year after year she wore black widow's clothes. Years of loneliness with no one to come after her, an empty promise never fulfilled. She endured a double dishonor: widowed twice, mother of none. All this from the family chosen by God supposedly to become the hope of the world.

Some of you have worn black for a long time too. The man who was supposed to love you didn't. The one who promised to be faithful wasn't. The family who should've protected you looked the other way. The wreckage of you was cast aside like Tamar—out of sight, out of mind. Surely, you'd move on. You'd get over it.

There is an excellent chance the apology you're waiting for isn't coming. That man will probably not show up on your doorstep, begging your forgiveness and confessing his mistakes. He might never own the pain he caused you or take steps toward reconciliation. His gut-wrenching remorse on your front porch one afternoon is an unlikely fantasy.

So you're still wearing black.

WHY WHITE IS THE NEW BLACK

Believer, hear Jesus' earnest pleading to a beloved, struggling church: "You have a reputation for being alive, but you are dead. Wake up! Strengthen what remains and is about to die" (Revelation 3:1-2). And for those who bravely obey? "They will walk with me, dressed in white, for they are worthy" (verse 4).

The color of the redeemed is white, dear one, and you don't have to wait for someone else's remorse to wear it. Even if you have a reputation for being alive, that bitterness will slowly kill you inside. That deadness will poison everything that remains if you refuse to throw off the black cloak of mourning.

So where does Jesus get off putting this responsibility on us? *Wake up? Strengthen what remains?* Who does He think we are? Does He understand what we've been through? "Wake up" sounds like "Get over it." Doesn't He care that we've been trying to get over it but it won't go away? It sits in our memories, reminding us of our injuries against the cold backdrop of the offender's indifference.

The answer lies in God's most ingenious invention: forgiveness. Of all His tools, this one is most misunderstood. We have the healing agent at our fingertips, and it has little to do with anyone being sorry. "When you refuse to forgive someone," wrote Henry Cloud and John Townsend in *Boundaries*, "you still want something from that person, and even if it is revenge that you want, it keeps you tied to him forever. [Forgiveness] ends your suffering, because it ends the wish for repayment that is never forthcoming and that makes your heart sick because your hope is deferred. Cut it loose, and you will be free."[5]

Unforgiveness is an iron chain that tethers you to a sinking ship. Unless you cut it loose, you will drown. But don't mistake forgiveness with denial. God never denies an injustice. When we hurt Him, He names it, He grieves it, He speaks His feelings about it. He doesn't declare it "okay" or "no big deal." Nor does He look the other way or brush it under the carpet. He deals with it, feels His feelings, then lets it go.

Forgiveness does not necessarily lead to reconciliation. God forgave the whole world of their sins, but not everyone is in relationship with Him. Why? They haven't owned their own sin yet. Forgiveness is one-sided. It happens in your heart when you release someone from the debt he owes you. You no longer condemn him. He is free from your anger.

And so are you.

You are worthy of a walk, arm in arm, with your Savior. He is the only man qualified to define you. It's time to wake up, throw off the mourning clothes. It's going to feel so good. Put on the white that becomes you. Strengthen what remains, and so much does, dear one: other relationships you've been blessed with, happy memories to make, your undeniable gifts, *the rest of your life.*

Wouldn't it be a relief to move on? Wouldn't you love to be rid of that bitterness? All that hurt? Release your disappointment; you're not condoning or excusing terrible behavior. Forgiveness doesn't mean it never happened; it simply means you won't go down with a sinking ship. Don't do it for him; do it for yourself.

In the next chapter, we'll see Tamar throw off *her* widow's clothes. Although we'll scratch our heads at the weirdness of her story, we'll see holy imagination and unlikely deliverance, too. Until then, let me pray this over you, my sweet friend:

Lord, for every woman who has been poorly defined by another, I pray Your affection to win her over. Lift her broken identity out of the rubble of human opinion and remind her of her heritage. She is loved. She is important. She is the apple of Your eye. Grant her the gift of perspective. Give her a moment in the shoes of another. Then empower her with another perspective: Yours. Restore her glory as Your daughter, as a treasure. Where she has been innocent, show her. Help us shed our black clothes of mourning for white robes of glory. Remind us that no man can strip us of our splendor; only one man was that powerful, and He made us perfect. Come, Jesus. Make it true in our lives.

CHAPTER 3

The Art of Calculation

Why I Love Smart Girls

Truth #1:

Women are terribly clever and intuitive.

GENESIS 38

So help me, I've had it. If I see another vacant, self-absorbed socialite carrying a little dog and posing for cameras with that practiced glance over the shoulder, I'm going to vomit. I would love to wrap my hands around their underfed little noodle necks and make them put their cleavages away and wear some underwear, because my daughter is a tween, and as God is my witness, the first time she speaks one adoring word about Britney, Paris/Nicole, Jessica, Christina, or "L.L.," it's only a matter of time before I'm named in a restraining order.

I commiserate with Celia Rivenbark over her daughter's graduating to the size 7–16 clothes department:

Just for old times' sake, I wandered through the 4–6X section. It was just an arm's length away, but it was the difference between a Happy Meal at the playground and bulimia at the bar. So far, these clothes had been left mercifully untouched by the wand of the skank fairy.

Instead of being able to buy pretty things for my daughter, sweet somethings in ice cream colors, I must now shop at big, boxy unisex stores where you can still buy shorts that don't say DELICIOUS on the bottom or T-shirts that are plain instead of a size 7 belly shirt with MADE YA LOOK on the front. Look at what? There's not supposed to be anything to look at on a seven-year-old. *Because they're children.*"[1]

One of my daughter's classmates wrote as her life's ambition, "To become an heiress." I couldn't make that up. Girls, when did dumb become fashionable? I missed the trend shift. While my friends and I were scraping together college tuition, the cute little girl from *The Parent Trap* remake garnered more influence than the president of the United States and became the Beacon of Boobs and Babbling for an entire generation.

I'm sorry I'm mean (I meant all that in the nicest way), but hell hath no fury like the mother of a daughter in American pop culture. Granted, I recognize slight similarities to my mom's irrational tirades against Madonna, but at least she grew up and wrote a children's book. Complete vindication for us daughters of the '80s, am I right? Trashy women don't write sweet books about roses and British people. (You were *so wrong* about her, Mom.)

Am I naïve to hope for a generation of role models to take their rightful places? The ones with the big brains and fierce intelligence? Then it dawns on me: That's us, girls. We are the generation they're watching. We are the ones choosing between substance and flash. We're helping the next group decide whether to spend their efforts fine-tuning the outside or inside.

My husband and I recently went to a wedding, where I spent time with my new friend Loren. She is blisteringly witty, and we thoroughly enjoyed our banter and sarcasm. She is the friend you instantly feel you've known your whole life. The next week, she sent me a two-line e-mail that said, "I really like you. You're funny and smart."

Gasp! *Funny and smart?!* I'll tell you right now, that is the finest compliment anyone could pay me. I never aspired to be the pretty girl or the party girl. That pretty face will wrinkle, and that partying contributes to the growing muffin-top. Humor and intellect are currencies infinitely more valuable to me.

I can see without question that God created His daughters with a stunning intelligence. We are not naïve, we are not helpless. We are not simply vessels of procreation. We are not just the oil that keeps the machine running. Women are capable of such brilliance, I am often rendered speechless as its witness.

BARKING IS FOR DOGS

As we move forward with Tamar, you'll see a streak of cleverness barely rivaled in God's Word. Conventional it is not, but God throws in His lot with those who don't exactly fit into the tightly righteous box. Jesus is far less predictable than His followers anyway.

Tamar was left in her father's house, twice widowed, awaiting Judah's youngest son, Shelah, to marry her. But she was not a dullard, and it was clear this was a futile wait. Judah would never send Shelah. Tamar must've had a watch party on her side, because Genesis 38:13 says, "Tamar was told, 'Your father-in-law is on his way to Timnah to shear his sheep.'" Someone had her back. This thing stunk to the high heavens, and somebody gave her the info she needed to formulate a plan: Judah's wife had died, and he and his buddy were coming her way.

Hmmm. What would you do, girls? What *do* we do when faced with obstacles and injustices? Let's lay our inferior strategies on the inspection table. Rather than activating intelligence, some women employ a masculine bite and lacerating tongue (not us, of course, but our friends). Instead of embracing our feminine problem-solving gifts, a male-oriented swagger makes its appearance.

But Lisa Bevere writes,

> Women acting like men could never possibly right these wrongs. Nor will we find our answers by attempting to reengineer or abandon the female gender. . . . In the past, women have been encouraged to prove themselves by fighting, seducing, or displacing the men to recapture a portion of their strength; but making men look weak has never made us look strong. No, this revelation and restoration can take place only as we return and rebuild the positions of authority and power already given to the woman by birthright.[2]

Neglecting our feminine smarts for a masculine bark is like mixing two colors of Play-Doh—after awhile it just all turns brown. Think of the woman who henpecks her husband within an inch of his sanity. A lifetime of yelling, criticizing, and dominating doesn't paint a nice picture of womanhood. Sure, she may get her way, but at what cost? This approach demeans one for the sake of the other. That doesn't solve the problem; it switches problems.

Rising up in domination only *seems* like a decent idea. When all else fails, right? That's the logic men historically used, and look where that got us. "The common belief—and in great part it's a reality—is that in light of the times and most of our personal circumstances, 'a woman's got to do what a woman's got to do' to survive," wrote Michelle McKinney Hammond in *The Power of Being a Woman.* "This is all part and parcel of what the sin factor delivers to our door. . . .When we lose ourselves as women and begin forcing ourselves to develop muscles we're not designed to have, our internal and relational system suffers."[3]

Hostile aggression no more works for a woman than for a man, and he becomes emasculated, losing affection for his partner. The relational rhythm we were trying for is destroyed by our methods. The whole thing smacks of a design problem. Perhaps we were created to communicate not with aggressive strength but with wisdom.

There is a better way.

"WORKS WELL WITH OTHERS"

Dr. Martin Luther King Jr. preached, "The aftermath of nonviolence is the creation of the beloved community. The aftermath of nonviolence is redemption. The aftermath of nonviolence is reconciliation. The aftermath of violence is emptiness and bitterness. . . . Let us never fight with falsehood and violence and hate and malice, but always fight with love."[4]

The crazy idea of submission might seem archaic for this problem. Even as I typed the "S" word, I heard you sigh. This is what I'm getting at: We always hear, "Wives, submit to your husbands as to the Lord" (Ephesians 5:22). But what about the verse before it?

"Submit to one another out of reverence for Christ."

Jesus introduced mutuality to unlock a prison cell. Remember, He created them male and female and blessed them. He blessed them both and equally. When one is elevated at the expense of the other, we have derailed. Fighting fire with fire means everyone gets charred. There should be a holy respect between men and women. It is faulty logic to drop the standard because "he did it first." If I'm engaged in battle with my five-year-old, lying on the floor and growling like he's doing won't solve the problem.

The lowest common denominator should not be our measure. Cooler heads often prevail with women. Untold tragedies were averted because a woman spoke rationally into a man's aggression. Wisdom always emerges the victor, preserving life and love and honor.

Right now my husband's blood pressure is probably rising and he has no idea why. This may shock you, but I have fire in my veins. I'm sure it's not coincidental that I married a maverick either. Our marriage is God's boot camp for His two passionate servants. *Passive* is not an adjective that gets wasted on either of us. It has taken much work ("takes" is the proper tense, really) to temper my mouth.

I often fail. The other day, we were discussing the speed-dial feature on our cell phones. In my casual commentary, I told Brandon that due to the Irrefutable and Universal Law of Speed Dial, voice mail was number one but, naturally, he was number two, followed by a long list of girlfriends. Obviously, the descending order mirrored my relational priorities, he occupying top billing in my heart.

That's when I noticed a cagey look on his face.

"What's your speed dial lineup?" I asked like the innocent dove I am, naïvely assuming that I, too, was way up in his ranking system, having birthed his children and been an absolute pleasure to live with these thirteen years.

That's when the bull began. "Oh yes, well, see, I was thinking I'd put you first, so I went ahead and put Tray second" (his number one boyfriend), "then I put in a couple of the fellas. About then I realized I couldn't put you first due to the Irrefutable and Universal Law of Speed Dial, but I was only at number six, and that didn't seem like a worthy number for my beautiful bride. So I put in one more and chose number seven for you. God's number. I'm honoring you."

I stared blankly, trying to channel my inner saint, but she'd gone missing, as she tends to do. "Are you saying I am number seven in your speed dial? And your five boyfriends took precedence over the woman who has sex with you? Do you think for one second I'm buying that crap you just fed me about putting me first? Do I look like some kind of half-wit? Hey, guess what, kids? Daddy is number one in my heart, and good news! Mommy slid in at number seven on Daddy's roster, just a hair ahead of his insurance agent! Maybe if I birth another namesake I can move up to number six!"

I'm still working on that wisdom thingy.

I'm not sure how rational intelligence would've responded. Perhaps it wouldn't have been overly sensitive and realized that the many sacrifices Brandon makes for me are somewhat indicative of his affection. Maybe it would've noted that speed dial, while a decent measuring tool, is perhaps not the end-all in prioritizing relationships. Maybe it would've thrown his cell phone in the toilet. I'm not sure.

THINGS THAT AREN'T SMART

What would intelligence do in Tamar's case? She had a dilemma maybe even worse than being number seven. Maybe a physical show of strength was in order. She could've ambushed Judah with stones and spears or leather sandals. (What *did* they have back then?) A hard slap across the face would've felt great too.

But an emotional attack probably stood a better chance. A vicious tongue-lashing could make stuff happen. A verbal assault might tip the scales in her favor if she exploited his guilt and delivered enough shame. A carefully targeted nag is highly underrated. Just wipe out a man with a tsunami of harassment.

Maybe she could've pulled her girlfriends into the attack like a gaggle of deranged seagulls. Together, they could embarrass him publicly enough to ensure some action. There's nothing like cutting a man's legs out from underneath him in front of his friends. That should get the wheels of justice turning. Men really respond to that.

Maybe she could've threatened a lawsuit, shown the authorities how Judah robbed her of her youth. Third-party interventions are good for scaring a man into right behavior. A well-placed threat goes far with the right delivery. Ultimatums are used not nearly enough against men, if you ask me.

These are tried-and-true methods of women. We've employed these tactics for centuries: physical aggression, emotional attacks, guilt mongering, nagging, gang warfare, public humiliation, threatening, ultimatums. Surely, one of them could've fixed Tamar's situation.

Which one did she choose?

HOOKERS AND HYPOCRITES

Yeah, about that. Here the story takes a turn. Upon hearing of Judah's journey in her direction, Tamar slipped off her widow's clothes, disguised herself with a veil, and sat on the road where Judah was passing. While that seems like innocuous information, understand that "veil disguise" meant "dressed like a hooker." Judah, bastion of honor, beelined toward her and said, "Come now, let me sleep with you."

Well, my stars. This guy. I can hardly stand the hypocrisy. What he denied Tamar through righteous means, he'd enjoy through immoral means. After all, he was a widower; can't expect him to go without forever. But Judah gets flattened by the irony truck.

Here our girl showed her true colors. "And what will you give me to sleep with you?" she asked innocently. Judah promised to send her a young goat—the bling-bling of ancient society. "Will you give me something as a pledge until you send it?" Tamar pressed gently. Judah, distracted by desire and anxious to get on with it, asked for a suggestion. These were trivial details standing in the way of his carnal needs (like foreplay, the plight of the modern man).

"Your seal and its cord, and the staff in your hand," recommended Tamar. Judah handed those over lickety-split, like a sex-crazed fool. A man's seal and cord were the ancient equivalent of a driver's license and Social Security card, used to seal documents and identify his family name. This was like a modern prostitute asking her client for his wallet. Let's just say that the only one thinking with her brain was Tamar.

A couple of days later, Judah sent his buddy back with the promised goat to retrieve his identification from "the shrine prostitute who was beside the road at Enaim." But the locals told him there was never any shrine prostitute. I'm sure they raised their eyebrows. Here's a guy with a goat, looking for a phantom hooker. That must've made a funny retelling later.

Judah panicked when he heard the news. "Let her keep what she has, or we will become a laughingstock." The KJV says, "Lest we be shamed." Ladies, God is constant; casual sex and the objectification of women were never acceptable. Of course, Judah was more concerned with embarrassment than with sin. His anxiety was about appearances, not holiness, as he declared, "Lest we be shamed," not "lest we be damned," as Matthew Henry noted.

Well, guess who turned up pregnant three months later? What his sons refused to accomplish, Judah did unwittingly. Get this, girls: Someone tattled to Judah, "Your daughter-in-law Tamar is guilty of prostitution, and as a result she is now pregnant." How did Judah, Dr. of Hypocrisy, respond? "Bring her out and have her burned to death!"

Can you even take it? It's like a scene from *Days of Our Lives*. You couldn't write this any tawdrier. But take heart, my friends: On God's watch, the worst wickedness—committed and concealed—is often strangely brought to light. Heading toward the stake, Tamar said simply,

"I am pregnant by the man who owns these. See if you recognize whose seal and cord and staff these are."

Oh. My. Land.

Can you imagine how Judah's stomach dropped? All eyes must've turned on the man who just called for her death sentence. What mandated her execution was right as rain for him. I bet he instantly recalled his words to his grieving father about Joseph: "We found this. Examine it to see whether it is your son's robe." His presentation concealed his sin, while Tamar's revealed it. Yet, in this moment, something shifted in Judah. His coldhearted indifference became a tender softening, and mercy cracked through.

"She is more righteous than I," he said quietly.

He never touched her again, and Tamar bore twin sons — one the head of the leading clan in Judah, the ancestor of David and ultimately of Christ. The narrator leaves us with the tension of wading through her dubious actions, neither condoning nor condemning them.

MIND PLUS HEART= SMART GIRL

Certainly, this drama is descriptive, not prescriptive. We won't teach our children to act like prostitutes and sleep with their fathers-in-law. But I wonder if there are seeds of godliness in Tamar's questionable scheme. She had two bad options: remain widowed and childless in her father's home, or make a risky, brazen, outrageous move and secure her due legacy. She chose the path with a kernel of righteousness in it, fulfilling the promise to Abraham she was a rightful heir of.

Judah acknowledged this in his concession, realizing that Tamar's desire to produce children put her nicely on God's covenant track. She, not Judah, acted like a descendant of Abraham. While Judah abandoned the kingdom, Tamar forced her way in. She exercised an intelligent tenacity, and because of her actions, Israel got its David and the world got its Christ.

Girls, while we rightly question Tamar's methods, we can learn from her approach. She totally engaged her brain. She weighed the crisis and invented the only solution a woman in her position had. Rather than leave her legacy to Judah—who'd proven unreliable—she constructed a clever plan and executed it. She chose holy imagination rather than passive resignation or hysteria.

What if we consulted our minds before our emotions? What if we chose reason over reaction? Some say men are brain-oriented and women are heart-oriented, but I find a disconnect there.

Wisdom makes our minds and hearts a unified front, one informing the other, neither eclipsing the other. Passionate intelligence and rational emotion are the greatest kingdom tools God gave women. We can size up a situation, discern the options, and make decisions not only on efficiency and practicality but also on justice and holiness.

Mind plus heart.

Deborah tempered Barak's fear with strategy, the universal language of men. Hannah challenged Eli's hasty judgment with faith; a beloved prophet was born. Esther countered King Xerxes' callousness with compassion; genocide was averted. Abigail calmed David's fury with wisdom; his legacy was preserved. All used shrewd approaches, deliberate communication.

No woman should check her brain at the door. Paul reminds us that as believers, "we have the mind of Christ" (1 Corinthians 2:16). Think of it: that brilliant mind of reconciliation and justice, wisdom and peacemaking. The mind of our Savior—we have it. His ability to level a trick question, His knack for knowing exactly how to proceed, His awareness of the big picture—Jesus is the pattern we were cut from.

I am more awed by Jesus' communication skills than by His

miracles. When I study His quick retorts and loaded questions, I cannot fathom how such a brilliant Savior chose a thief's dishonorable death for me. He was a dazzling thinker, a Man among boys. I have begged for one molecule of Jesus' genius to infect my teaching, my responses, my problem-solving skills. To reflect a fraction of His passionate intelligence is my life's goal. Yet my Hero tells me, "Anyone who has faith in me will do what I have been doing. He will do even greater things than these" (John 14:12).

We are smart and savvy, and only the confused woman forfeits these qualities in deference to a man. Submission is not constructed upon a woman's silence. Countless spiritual heroes would've self-destructed if not for the intelligent intervention of women in their lives, not to mention women who are spiritual giants themselves, champions of faith.

A woman of wisdom is a centrifugal force, drawing everyone into her. She weighs her words before answering. Her counsel is unbreakably linked to God's principles. She is sought out, respected, heeded. How many sons and daughters seek their mothers' guidance? How many young brides learn from an older wife?

It is no surprise that wisdom is named a "she" in Proverbs:

> Does not wisdom call out?
>> Does not understanding raise her voice? . . .
> Listen, for I have worthy things to say;
>> I open my lips to speak what is right.
> My mouth speaks what is true,
>> for my lips detest wickedness. . . .
> I, wisdom, dwell together with prudence;
>> I possess knowledge and discretion." (Proverbs 8:1,6-7,12)

Knowledge with discretion — mind plus heart — is a mighty force.

If you evaluated your most pressing issue right now, what would wisdom say? Would you parent differently if you tempered your affection with logic? How would intelligence advise your troubled relationship? Would the mind of Christ strike a better balance between acting out of woundedness versus reason?

Often the smart answer eludes us, because our emotions blur it. Rather than give our feelings a dictatorship over our actions, we should sit them down with reason, intuition, and prudence and let them have a roundtable discussion. Together, they'll know what to do.

John put it like this: "We have seen his glory, the glory of the One and Only, who came from the Father, full of *grace* and *truth*" (1:14, emphasis added). Grace without truth becomes lascivious, while truth without grace becomes oppressive. The marriage of the two mimics our Savior. He never sacrificed one for the other. His brain and heart collaborated on every word.

Can you imagine how our lives would look if we figured this out?

JESUS, DO YOU THINK I'M SMART? CHECK YES OR NO.

This is to say nothing of the teachings, visions, missions, creativity, and ridiculous talents we effect. Women are some of the smartest people on earth. Our intelligence is not simply a road map through our relationships; it is the raw material for the work of our hands, and as David pointed out, "What is man that you are mindful of him, the son of man that you care for Him? You made him ruler over the works of your hands."

We are the hands of God on this planet. While we blame God for letting things get so bad, He says *we* are His answer. "Over and over, when I ask God why all of these injustices are allowed to exist in the world," wrote Shane Claiborne in *The Irresistible Revolution*, "I can feel the Spirit whisper to me, 'You tell me why we allow this to happen. You are my body, my hands, my feet.'"[5]

It is not Christlike to shrink in subservience or cower in insecurity. Some women wait indefinitely for a man, another woman, anyone else to fix things, start things, dream things. She doesn't acknowledge her intellect or her ability to implement it. There is no sense of initiative, no stirrings of vision. Had this been Tamar's position, she would've died a widow in her father's house, having no part in the lineage of Christ.

Through her story, I am inspired with challenge and resolve. Some of us need to hand over the helpless card and stand on the two good legs God gave us. It's time to activate our smarts and instead of waiting for a solution, *become the solution*. I have been exposed to the most clever, creative, resourceful women you could imagine. In the face of injustice and impossible obstacles, they embraced their mind of Christ and became His hands in the process. I look forward to telling their stories in the last chapter.

GOD CAN FIX BAD GUYS

I want to wrap up Tamar's story. From highly embarrassing beginnings emerged a lovely picture of redemption. Tamar was welcomed into the lineage of Christ despite her questionable methods, to say nothing of her being a Canaanite. God accepts the unsightly edges of the good-hearted. He is quick to respond to what's good in us and slow to react to what isn't.

Let's not forget Judah, that old troublemaker. I am learning to love how God is passionate about the oppressed *and* the oppressor. Dr. King spoke of it in racial terms: "Our aim must never be to defeat or humiliate the white man. We must not become victimized with a philosophy of black supremacy. God is not interested merely in freeing black men and brown men and yellow men, but God is interested in freeing the whole human race."[6]

We kind of want Judah to get what's coming to him. He behaved badly, and he belongs on God's Naughty List. Frankly, he doesn't deserve grace. But who does? Tamar's behavior wasn't exactly pristine either. See, God's first bent is mercy. He longs to liberate the victim from her oppression, and the oppressor from his confusion. When either emerges transformed, it is a victory for the heavens.

Judah changed the day his seal and cord indicted him. The cold, calculating Judah was reformed into a tender, wise ancestor of Jesus. Every biblical account of Judah from that point is righteous. God is not vindictive, no matter what you've heard. He confronts us with our sin not to condemn us but to redeem us.

In fact, outside of "Son of David," the only other human name identified with Jesus is "Lion of the Tribe of Judah." Out of the rubble of immorality rose triumph. God accounted for Judah's terrible abdication and Tamar's disgraceful means, and he stuck with them both.

So who emerges as the real hero in this story? Certainly not Judah. Tamar is flawed, at best. I offer, then, that the real Hero is the Lord Himself, the God of Abraham, Isaac, and Jacob; the God who wasn't deterred by the failings of His chosen man; the God who didn't disqualify a young woman due to her schemes but instead covered both with grace, mercy, and loyal love.

Though we wouldn't exactly emulate either character, we discover we *are* like them. We make mistakes. We operate out of fear and selfishness. We make decisions we wish we had back. We leave people in the wake of our agendas. We make a general mess of things.

Then we see that somehow, in some miraculous way, God manages to accomplish something good no matter how undeserving we are. Being on the receiving end of grace is always surprising. If we, like Tamar, are startled to find our names in the family tree of Jesus, adopted into this holy community in spite of everything we've done to disqualify ourselves, well, it's further proof that God's love is so deep and unshakeable that we cannot comprehend it this side of heaven. Maybe one day when we stand with the murderers and prostitutes and liars and cowards who comprise the family of God, we'll finally grasp the depth of mercy that brought us there.

And we'll bow to the Lion of the Tribe of Judah.

CHAPTER 4

A Bunch of Reduced Fractions

Does God Use Only Whole Numbers?

Myth #2:

Our history can be only a little bad.

JOSHUA 2

I wonder what it's like to be a graceful woman who never sticks her foot in her big, stupid mouth? Oh, to be a gentle sage who never lies in bed recounting all the people she shocked that day! Well, girls, I'll never know.

Take, for instance, "The Mexican Debacle," as it is now known. We served a young guy named Luis while still doing college ministry. He and Brandon were particularly close, and God developed Luis's heart for missions during those years. After graduation, he accepted a long-term mission assignment in Mexico.

Know this about Luis: He was 100 percent Hispanic, but he knew zero Spanish, talked like a surfer, and dressed like an Abercrombie model. When he attempted Spanish, it was only slightly better than George W. This provided a steady stream of comedy for everyone, Luis included. He always joked about the chasm between his heritage and reality.

I should underscore our affinity before telling you what I said about him:

- He was baptized by Brandon.
- He babysat our kids.
- He interned for my husband.
- He spent the better part of six years with our family.
- *We loved him.*

That said, our friends hosted a send-off party before Luis left for Mexico. This was a spiritual occasion where his friends and family could pray over him and commission him to the ministry. His Spanish-speaking mother, brother, and family traveled to Austin for the send-off. It was a holy gathering.

I took my plate into the room where we were eating. I sat next to Luis's sweet mother and launched into a rant on why we loved him so. But often with me, one renegade sentence separates itself from the pack of godliness I'm delivering, and it gets impatient and runs ahead of its righteous friends and bursts out before I can identify it as U.I. (utterly inappropriate). And before I am even aware of its existence in my brain, it makes its shocking appearance like a streaker at a graduation ceremony.

Because, honest to goodness, I looked at this dear woman and said, "Luis is the whitest Mexican we've ever known!"

These are the words that came out of my mouth.

By a stroke of divine intervention, my husband was not in the room, because he would've passed out in his fajitas. I did manage, however, to grind the table conversation to a screeching halt while everyone sat in stunned silence, incapable of breaking the awkward racial spell I'd just cast.

I stared pleadingly at my Girlfriend Steph, but she was too frozen in an ice block of horror to rescue me. I began babbling incoherently, trying to undo the damage, but it got worse before it got better, which was never. My friend Mark told me later, "I've never heard anyone insult a woman's heritage *and* her children in so few words. That was amazing."

Sadly, I have a thousand stories like that one. The people left in my verbal wake are legion. The scary thing is, it's not getting any better. I keep thinking that any day I'll wake up with a developed sense of judgment, yet I keep saying stuff like, "Luis is the whitest Mexican we've ever known."

You can see why I am floored that God would do business with me. *As a communicator.* There are so many other women better than I am. So many who don't pose a legitimate threat to His kingdom. So many who don't begin their morning conference sessions with the same tired line: "Let me apologize for something I said in our session last night . . ."

Sometimes I don't know what to make of God. Doesn't this Guy have any standards? Fortune 500 companies succeed by hiring qualified visionaries with a history of achievement. They look at professional accomplishments and education pedigree and select the finest candidates, and then everything they touch turns to gold because they are so dang capable.

Yet the God of the universe—supposedly the smartest Guy ever—takes the exact opposite approach for His staff. He selects the most awkward, unqualified, tainted vessels, and then assigns them world-changing visions they seem incapable of executing. What is with this Guy? Should we be thrilled or terrified that this is His business model?

DESERT WANDERING WAS FOR SUCKERS

Maybe the next woman in Jesus' lineage will clear this up. About four hundred years go by until we reach the next of Christ's female ancestors mentioned in Matthew. In that time, Abraham's family grew to a nation of two million in Egypt, where they originally traveled to visit that brother who Judah sold into slavery. That stopover cost them, because the Egyptians decided these Hebrews made better slaves than citizens. For around 350 years, they were enslaved.

As the story goes, God raised Moses up to deliver them from bondage. Burning bush, ten plagues, Passover, Red Sea, yada yada yada. After they received the Law, it was time to enter the Promised Land. This was God's plan—to usher them straight from slavery to freedom with just enough lag time to receive their new operating rules. So Moses formed an espionage team to case the nearest city. His protégé, Joshua, and eleven others went on a reconnaissance mission, barely one year after crossing the Red Sea.

But of the twelve spies, only Joshua and Caleb trusted God's sovereignty enough to back a Hebrew invasion. The rest shrunk in fear and spread terror throughout the people. So God declared that of every adult who witnessed His miraculous deliverance from Egypt, only Joshua and Caleb would enter the Promised Land. Thus, forty years of homelessness commenced, while the adult community slowly died out. Every time I read this story, I hope for a different ending, but Moses was also barred from entering the P. L. He died just across the river from it, because of a glitch in obedience. (I wanted him to make it in so bad.)

In his place, God commissioned Joshua, one of the two faithful spies.

So after forty years, we find Joshua and the two million Hebrews east of the Jordan River, five miles from the major Canaanite city, Jericho. God delivered a beautiful speech about courage and faithfulness, and Joshua knew it was time. Again.

Obviously, Joshua was aware of the power of an advance scout team. They would either be the front door into this land, or they could activate another forty years of wandering. Like Moses, he sent men into Jericho, but rather than twelve spies, he chose two; the other ten were deadweight last time. Quite literally, he was putting all their eggs in this basket. Four decades ago, the spiritual failure of the spies was catastrophic.

Here's the deal with Jericho, though. Historical and archaeological accounts show that Jericho was terribly fortified. It was encircled by towering double walls fifteen feet apart, rising "up to the sky," according to the prophets and patriarchs. It was the strongest fortress in the land and, naturally, the first one God wanted them to conquer. You know He's like that.

One last note before we meet our girl. Jericho, like every city in the Middle East then, was completely pagan. It was dominated by idol worship, primarily fertility gods like Baal and Ashtoreth. A study of ancient ruins shows Canaan's rich material culture, and evidence of immoral behavior and cruelty is clear. Pagan temples, altars, tombs, and ritual vessels have been uncovered and shed light on their culture and customs.[1] Though God's name was becoming famous in the region, He had no honor in Jericho.

WHAT IS IT WITH GOD AND PROSTITUTES?

"'Go, look over the land, especially Jericho,' Joshua secretly told the two spies. So they went and entered the house of a prostitute named Rahab and stayed there."

Let's stop there, because this is the next honoree in Jesus' lineage. Does it give you pause that the first woman named in Jesus' line acted like a prostitute, and the second woman *was* one? To be sure, Rahab was a prostitute in the dirtiest sense of the word. Josephus, Jewish historian of the first century, discreetly called her "an innkeeper."[2] Another scholar heralded her as "a single woman who obtained an honest livelihood."[3]

People, please. *Prostitute* is from the Hebrew word *zanah.* The Greek Old Testament translation uses the word *porne,* which also means a harlot. It is from a group of words meaning "commit fornication" or "act immorally." It is where we derive the word pornography. Let there be no doubt: Rahab was a hooker, and not a cult prostitute in the temple but a backroom fornicator.

But allow me to defend her. Then and now, prostitution is a moral issue to outsiders, but it's an economic issue to insiders. No girl dreams of becoming a hooker. This is the plight of the desperate. Would we condemn girls sold into sex trafficking for acting immoral? The teenager kicked out and left to streetwalking as lustful? These are daughters, sisters, mothers. They had dreams once.

We read later of Rahab's parents and siblings, yet she is turning tricks. Customarily, her family would provide for her, so we assume she is supporting them. Were they plagued with poverty? Landlessness? A handicap or debilitating injury? Were they social pariahs? The Bible is silent on that, but it was uncommon for a woman with living parents and brothers to choose this vocation. This was a last option for the hopeless.

Who among us can't understand that? Perhaps you've made choices out of desperation too. I'm certain the mother who aborted her baby understands; so does the abused girl who struggled with promiscuity. I bet the unloved daughter can relate; she probably behaved out of an affection vacuum. The secret addict gets it; her pain fuels her private struggle. She never wanted this battle. I'm sure the neglected wife floundering in an affair understands; she wouldn't have written her script like this.

NO LOVE FOR THE RAHABS

It's easy for the self-righteous to condemn desperate women. Just pluck the behavior out of its context and it's a simple matter of right and wrong. Prostitution, abortion, promiscuity, substance abuse, adultery, homosexuality—bad girls. Tsk, tsk. Such tainted vessels. They just couldn't swim in the good-choices pool. So their hearts are overlooked for their actions. It's much easier. Dealing with their circumstances is too messy for the average saint.

Sexual history is a dark covering for women. There's sin, then there's *that kind of sin*. These transgressions are a sticking point for those partaking and those judging. They invoke an extra measure of disgrace, regardless of the circumstances, whether "ashamed of" or "shame on."

Society has grace for insecurity and anger management; give us a woman struggling with motherhood or depression. But sexual indiscretion? That's too dirty for God to deal with, much less His followers trying to be holy. Perhaps this is why Josephus called Rahab an innkeeper—he just couldn't honor a sexually polluted woman. Her history had to be propped up to make it fit.

Is there hope for the Rahabs?

Charles Spurgeon preached (I'll convert the *thee*'s, *thou*'s, and *thine*'s),

Take comfort. The same faith which saved Rahab can save you. Are you literally one of Rahab's sisters in guilt? She was saved, and so may you be, if God shall grant you repentance. Woman! Are you loathsome to yourself? Do you stand at this moment in this assembly, and say, "I am ashamed to be here; I know I have no right to stand among people who are chaste and honest"? I bid you still remain; yes, come again and make this your Sabbath house of prayer. You are no intruder! You are welcome! For you have a sacred right to the courts of mercy. You have a sacred right; for here sinners are invited.[4]

LOVE FOR THE RAHABS

Dear one, you are loved by a Savior with a special affinity for prostitutes and the like. Of the five women named in His lineage, three of them were sexually corrupted. He ate with hookers, consorted with them, defended them, redeemed them. He seemed to understand that the darkest sins come from the deepest hurts.

Jesus considers the heart before the habit, which is why the Pharisees were never commended for their impeccable behavior. His first concern is motive; behavior is second. He considers the pain, abuse, neglect, or fear that fuels poor conduct, and He won't accept spotless adherence to the rules without holy intentions.

God seems to pick jacked-up people on purpose. Evidently, where sin abounds, grace abounds all the more. He thinks those who are forgiven much will love much. He chooses the weak things of the world intentionally, because it seems that what is sown in dishonor is raised in glory (or so goes the Bible's telling of it).

There is no such thing as too messed up for God. Frankly, the more stained you are, the more likely you'll be selected for service. Sinners and fools are God's first choices. Shane Claiborne wrote of a talk he gives called "The Scandal of Grace," in which he discusses God's love for Osama bin Laden, Saddam Hussein, Saul of Tarsus, Timothy McVeigh, and himself. He shows a film with images behind the words *amazing grace that saved a wretch like me*, and different faces are branded with the words *like me* including some notorious evildoers just mentioned.

At one church, the film created such discomfort that the program team removed the image of Timothy McVeigh before the second service. "There is something scandalous about grace," Claiborne wrote. "It's almost embarrassing that God loves losers so much."[5]

This is such good news to me. While it means a selfish coward like me ends up writing books and teaching for Jesus (which should scare us all), it also means that tainted vessels are welcome in God's family. We cannot disqualify ourselves from grace—I don't care what you've done or where you are.

After years of being a hopeless legalist, I now adore the gap between salvation and God's next movement of liberation in a woman's life. It is a beautiful revelation that mercy has one prerequisite, one partner in the work of redemption, and that is faith—not merit, not playing nice, not a promise to be good.

KEEPING OUT THE CRAZIES (HELPING JESUS OUT)

I'm sure some of my dear readers are fretting, wringing their hands at the absurd gospel of grace. Where is the holiness? Where is the good behavior? Are we to accept anyone? Does no one have to toe the line anymore?

Donald Miller addressed this tension in *Blue Like Jazz*:

I was a fundamentalist Christian once. It lasted a summer. I was in that same phase of trying to discipline myself to "behave" as if I loved light and not "behave" as if I loved darkness. I used to get really ticked about preachers who talked too much about grace, because they tempted me to not be disciplined. I figured what people needed was a kick in the butt, and if I failed at godliness it was because those around me weren't trying hard enough. I believed if word got out about grace, the whole church was going to turn into a brothel. I was a real jerk, I think.[6]

What kind of gospel is this? It's nothing more than a sanctuary for the wicked, where the worst people are absolved of their actions. What kind of God doesn't hold anything against anyone just for their asking? The good news is this: The gospel is indeed a refuge for liars, murderers, cowards, and prostitutes; adulterers, bigots, thieves, and betrayers; the weak, pathetic, hateful, and hopeless. But it is a hospital, too, because it heals us of our sins, binds up our wounds, and delivers us from our diseases. Once we enter, we are eternally changed. The sanctuary becomes a hospital that turns into a home.

God chose Rahab while she was still turning tricks, but He didn't leave her there.

CONFESSIONS OF AN OUTCAST

My son Gavin was seven when he took his first and last venture into karate. I was a karate-class virgin, but still. I'm not sure that excuses our first day in the club. Having purchased his costume, or whatever it's called, we went to class. Evidently, I am incapable of reading a schedule, though, because instead of coming to the seven-year-old, beginners, boys-with-slight-ADHD-tendencies class, we showed up for the open class, which included any karate kid good or diligent enough to want more practice than my average boy, who was just there to become "a vicious warrior."

This misstep was made worse because we'd already managed to lose his precious white belt when he used it as some sort of "whapper" in the forest behind our house. I suggested letting his robe flap open like Hugh Hefner, but this was unacceptable. So I did what any mom would do: I took my daughter's off-white, knit sweater belt (with only teeny pink embroidered roses) and tied up his outfit thing.

I marched my son in semi-drag into his first class with boys twice his age, let my other two roll around on the karate floor, and tried not to watch Gavin making muscle poses in the mirror while everyone else did their tricks. Five minutes later, a karate mom marched over and said with distaste, "It dishonors the art to be on the mat with shoes on. Your children need to remove their flip-flops and bow before stepping onto the floor."

Well, what fresh hell is this? I'd discovered a whole new environment to be the Lucille Ball character in. Hopefully, this mom hadn't equated me with the kid in the second row doing Jackie Chan choreography and making grunting noises like an injured warthog.

At the end, when Gavin sauntered over with his sister's belt tied around his head like Rambo, the teacher walked over with him. I sensed my opportunity to show honor, respect, homage, and reverence for the art of karate.

"Bow to your sensei, Gavin," I commanded humbly.

"That's not what I'm called."

"My bad. Um, well, Gavin had a great time at karate!"

"It's Kuk Sool Won," he deadpanned.

"Well, it's been Kuk Sool Fun!"

That was the moment I backed out the door, having heaped so much dishonor on the craft that it might never recover. Needless to say, I became "that mom" in karate circles—I mean Kuk Sool Won circles. I never made it into their good graces, either. My grasp of protocol barely improved, and I started dropping him off rather than sitting under the weight of everyone's disapproval. No one missed us when we defected to soccer, I'm sure. You can't imagine how thrilled the soccer community is to have us, though . . .

I have a soft spot for outcasts. I've been an outsider so many times. I was too shy, then too loud. I wasn't cute enough. Not developed enough for the boys, then too developed for the girls. Not thin enough. Not pretty enough. Too pretty for them ("she must be vain"). Too Christiany here. Not Christiany enough there. Too young for this group. Too old for that group. Too conservative for those. Too liberal for them. Not enough money to run with this bunch. Not experienced in their area. Not acceptable for that crowd. Life sometimes seems like a game of *Who's In and Who's Out?*

Be certain that Rahab was out. Prostitutes were not outlawed, but they were outcast. She lived in a cramped space in the wall of Jericho, the refuge of the rejected. She was exposed to dirty, diseased men and viewed with distaste by society. She was the girl other women cut their eyes at. Rahab was surely never invited to weddings or celebrations; she was not included in the cultural happenings and events. Her community probably treated her how prostitutes are treated today. It's the oldest profession in the world.

I love the wording of the Bible: "So they went and entered the house of a prostitute named Rahab and stayed there." What do we have here? Lying down on the job? Some personal business before all the espionage? Did they mistake her house for city hall? Perhaps she stored the defense strategies and engineering documents they needed? Oh, all right, I'm just kidding. I don't actually believe they were there to get their kicks.

The Bible is silent on why they ended up at a prostitute's house. It's an awkward omission at best. But here is what I think: Based on the rest of the story, I believe that God looked on Jericho and found one friend of Israel, one heart inclined toward His sovereignty, and that was Rahab. Her current status was irrelevant to a God who needed an ally.

WHY DID *SHE* MAKE VARSITY?

More interesting is this: In their encounter with Rahab, which we'll talk about in the next chapter, no vital reconnaissance was uncovered. No essential information was gained to give the Hebrews an advantage in battle. Nothing was learned of Jericho's military prowess, nor was

Rahab central to their victory. It appears the story would've progressed like it did without this encounter at all. You could pluck her character out, and the ensuing drama would've carried on no differently. In fact, it seems an insignificant inclusion compared to the epic events that preceded and followed it.

Like with so many other questionable characters in Scripture (see the previous two chapters and the next five), we get access to their stories for what they teach us about God. Since there was a God to embrace, His followers have boxed Him in. We've confused His holiness as a barrier from humanity, at least from those who might offend His conscience. So Christianity leveled into The Worthy, The Minor Sinners, and The Embarrassing Sinners.

This story highlights the difference between human expectations and divine decisions. We meet Rahab so God can explain *His* criteria: "The eyes of the Lord move over all the earth so that He may give strength to those whose whole heart is given to Him" (2 Chronicles 16:9, NLV). Somehow this has become white noise in Scripture, totally irrelevant today.

When is the last time a dirty homeless man was welcomed into your church service, not just its food pantry? What if a hooker aligned herself with your women's ministry? What if God selected someone like Rahab to deliver His Word or His people? Who would listen to her? We'd be so uncomfortable with her sin, it would be a matter of "Someone deal with this so we can get rid of her."

Rahab's story is beautiful news to the Rahabs but often not welcomed by the pew fillers. Redemption is for everyone, not just those who seem worthy. That often necessitates a period between debauchery and liberation. Can you fathom how many live in that gap? Can you see how many souls are left on the proverbial salvation table when Christians won't stand by — much less love — another so broken?

It is a short step into grace; Jesus made it so simple. The divide is no greater for a prostitute than for a preacher's daughter. Often all a person needs is one friend to show her the way, but we are too preoccupied with "speaking truth," "rebuking," and "being set apart" to make contact with anyone under our spiritual rank. Had this been God's position, the Bible would be half its length; we'd be left with tabernacle dimensions in the Old Testament, and much of the New Testament would be thrown out because it was written by a reformed terrorist.

AMAZING GRACE THAT SAVED A WRETCH LIKE ME (BUT MAYBE NOT YOU)

God looked at Rahab and saw a fragile faith in a land of idolatry, and it was enough for Him. We *must* allow that fact to translate to our twenty-first-century existence. If you're stuck on the side of Rahab, it is your responsibility to receive your divine pardon. Rahab could've shut the door on those Hebrews, but instead she began a fantastical adventure with God to which we bear witness this day. It was a scary proposition, as we'll get into next, but I suspect her emancipation was well worth it.

It seems chilling to confront the God of the universe when your history (or current life) is dubious. Commiserate with any believer; she's been there, since there is no other pathway into salvation. Yet it is a choice to reject forgiveness—it's the only way not to receive it. Forgiveness is available. It is free. It is a gift. It has no prerequisites, save faith. God does not judge our future by everything we've done in the past. It's time we joined Him in that line of thinking.

Receive grace.

Move on.

And if you are already delivered from the toxic sins that ailed you, you have two mandates: One, never, never, not for a moment forget where you came from. A growing faith tempts us to shift the credit from a sacrificial Savior to our diligent efforts. Grace becomes fuzzy, a piece of our spiritual history that lost its significance. Stunningly, the staples of forgiveness, freedom, mercy, and redemption grow stale when outpaced by legalism.

Two, never, never, not for a moment become disgusted or apathetic about those who haven't found their spiritual footing. Your love for them doesn't turn into a sin endorsement. It is unnecessary to stay aloof on principle. The only statement believers make when they remain insulated is that they are judgmental elitists who prefer condemnation over love. Think I'm being harsh? Ask anyone on the receiving end of that behavior.

Love is the magic bullet that lifts broken people out of their pits — the love of their Creator, the love of their Savior, and the love of His people. Discipleship, reform, repentance — those will come. But we can't expect a prostitute to get a grip on holiness before she experiences forgiveness. Through our proximity and compassion, we represent Jesus accurately. It's a daunting notion that unbelievers equate God's voice with the Christians they hear.

What are they hearing from you?

I realize I've dived only two verses into this story. As I considered Rahab's tale, I realized that her tawdry history was too essential to skim. It's central to God's kingdom and, consequently, our involvement in it. As always, the Bible is a relief. Granted, His people are launched into one dangerous adventure after another, but give me an adventure with God any day over stagnation under His supposed condemnation.

If Rahab is welcomed, then so am I.

And so are you.

Let the adventure begin.

CHAPTER 5

Exponentiation

The Gospel of Jesus and Oprah

Truth #2:

Women are brave risk-takers.

Joshua 2

You can hardly fault my dad. What's a sports guy to do when he gets three daughters in a row? I'll tell you what: put softball gloves in their cribs so they develop the smell for dirty leather. He dressed his oldest daughter like a baseball player for her first Halloween and ironed "DLP" onto her hat (Daddy's Little Pitcher). He made that same daughter practice in the backyard until she caught twenty-five pop flies in a row, though the sun had set and she was at risk for a severe head injury or emotional breakdown.

But the worst happened in the summer of 1986.

Understand that my dad wanted me to be a fast-pitch softball pitcher in the same way others wanted their daughters to become surgeons. The summer I turned twelve, my dad heard that a pitching camp for girls was coming to Louisiana. It was taught by a legend who had coached at college and professional levels for forty years. It was labor-intensive. It was expensive. It was at Nichols State University in Thibodaux. Here's the critical part: It was for advanced pitchers in high school and college.

Guess who was in seventh grade?

Even worse, each pitcher brought her own catcher, which makes perfect sense for a competitive high school champ or Division I starter. These are girls that actually "have a catcher." My catcher? Dad. I'm not even kidding. There we were, father/daughter combo extraordinaire, to hear him describe it, walking toward the field on the first morning. Not only was I the youngest girl there by at least four years but any of them could've rolled me into a seventh-grade ball, pitched me to "her catcher," and then eaten me. I'm pretty sure half of them were dudes.

"I don't want to stay, Dad."

That comment was completely ignored, and we walked over to the group. I was so intimidated I could barely stand. Mercifully, the coach did not acknowledge me or do a special welcome for the youngest attendee, because I would've had a seizure. I remember contemplating how to break an ankle or pop my shoulder out of joint so we could leave. But before I properly developed a scheme, we began warming up.

And, by golly, that competitive edge my dad instilled kicked in. I listened to the coach's analysis of my mechanics and adjusted accordingly. Day after day, I pitched, fine-tuned, spit (trying to be like the girls), and pitched some more. Surprisingly, the man-girls encouraged me, sharing the experiences they had at my age. I began losing my fear and finding my passion again—after all, I loved this sport.

By the end, I'd received the coach's endorsement—which I suspect he gave to make "my catcher's" year, his paternal enthusiasm somewhat obvious—and forged friendships with the big girls. I took home valuable instruction I remember to this day. (Unfortunately, the coach prescribed one hundred pitches a day rain or shine to stay competitive, so I became a shortstop, which doesn't do much for this story.)

But here's the point: That summer I learned:

1. Girls can be brave, even when they're scared.
2. Sometimes an opportunity must be seized, even if you're out of your league.

Granted, this was a small stage to learn these lessons on, but aren't they still true when faced with unexpected single motherhood? A child in crisis? An injustice that can't be ignored? A divine assignment that will end your days of comfort? Every woman encounters such a moment, when you either shrink in fear or step forward in courage. You understand that either way you go, life will never be the same.

As we move on with Rahab, we'll find inspiration from her story and similar obstacles we face today. In some ways we are all Rahabs, and hopefully we'll discover her bravery seeded in our hearts too. I am proud to call her a sister, and I aim to be just like her (minus the brothel).

"THESE HOMELESS PEOPLE SCARE ME" — JERICHO

Go back with me to Jericho. We know from Rahab's later commentary that the city was painfully aware of the Hebrews. It's hard to miss two million wanderers camped five miles away. She told the spies later,

"I know that the LORD has given this land to you and that a great fear of you has fallen on us, so that all who live in this country are melting in fear because of you. We have heard how the LORD dried up the water of the Red Sea for you when you came of Egypt, and what you did to Sihon and Og, the two kings of the Amorites east of the Jordan, whom you completely destroyed. When we heard of it, our hearts melted and everyone's courage failed because of you."

There was a serious buzz in Jericho. People were freaking out. Word on the street was that this God of the Hebrews had promised them Jericho. Crazy rumors flew around for years about the parting of the Red Sea and the Hebrews' escape from Egypt. Lookouts reported their trek toward the Jordan, where they now camped. Imagine if a mystical people that size were minutes from your city, poised to conquer it.

Yet logistics and common sense were on Jericho's side. This was a double-fortified city with an organized, mobilized military. Breaching their walls was impossible. Archaeological excavations reveal continuous occupation at Jericho back to 7000 BC. Many battles had come and gone, and it remained unconquered. Plus, these Hebrews had wandered the desert for forty years, and most were women and children. They were hardly a military threat. Their recent victories against Sihon and Og were flukes; those were unfortified cities.

These up-and-down thoughts would've coursed through their minds. However, conventional wisdom would've sided with Jericho. Of the two opponents, the rational person wouldn't fancy her chances with a ragtag group of homeless people.

Knock, knock, knock.

There stood two Hebrew men at Rahab's door.

GOD KNOCKS AS OFTEN AS A JEHOVAH'S WITNESS

Can you fathom her dilemma? For what possible reason would she open that door? The better option was immediately exposing them to gain military protection or favor from the king, who might lift her out of her unfortunate circumstances, to say nothing of the consequences of helping them—treason is something of a sticking point. Were they dangerous? Would they hurt her? There wasn't a single reason to invite them in.

Well, I guess if you believed in God there was—which she did.

Siding with God's agenda rarely makes conventional sense. There are generally forty reasons on the con side and about two on the pro side, maybe one and a half. The obstacles look insurmountable. Resistance is guaranteed. The plan feels sketchy at best, if you even receive the whole plan. The risks seemingly outweigh the benefits. Oh, and failure appears imminent. Yay, God!

Yet He knocks.

"Hi! It's Me—God. Good morning! My name is Spiritual Assignment. Join Me. Side with Me. Be My hands and feet. Deliver My message. Accept this task. Be the voice of justice. Fight these enemies. Advocate for the oppressed. Tackle this problem. I have a project for you . . ."

I remember a notable knock: "Good afternoon! I'd like you to write a book on studying My Word. I realize that your children are one, three, and five and you have no child care or assistance. I understand that you haven't showered in three days and are wearing the same clothes as yesterday. No, you haven't been published. True, you have no literary connections or even a basic idea of what you're doing. Right, no one would have any reason to read anything you write. So see? Now's the perfect time, and you are the ideal candidate!"

Trust me, I thought about shutting the door in God's nice, optimistic face. Can you believe how crazy He is? This was His worst plan ever. That was April 2004. That November, I had a contract on a completed book, plus four more they assumed I could write.

I can't overstate how unqualified I was. Still am. I wonder

constantly if this is the day I'll get exposed. I warned God, "Someone will be on to me eventually, You know, and I'm blaming You." Yet here we are, on book number six. Conferences keep asking me to speak, like in front of people. None of this makes sense, believe me. There are so many reasons this should've failed, so many statistics that worked against me, so many women better than I am.

The only explanation I can offer is that God had an agenda and it was getting done. He overcomes guaranteed obstacles—the ones where everyone, everywhere is saying, "This can't work." There is no other explanation.

What assignment is He knocking on your door with?

YOU ARE A BIG FAT ANSWER

When God considers a task, He searches for a friend of the kingdom to join the fight. Who is willing? Who will be His ally on the ground? Who is up for a great adventure? If we decline, He'll knock on the next door. Like Mordecai told Esther, "If you remain silent at this time, relief and deliverance for the Jews will arise from another place, but you and your father's family will perish. And who knows but that you have come to royal position for such a time as this?" (Esther 4:14).

"You are somebody's answer," wrote Lisa Bevere. "You are something's answer. There is a problem out there only your presence can solve. There is a broken and wounded heart to which only you can administer healing. You are a voice to the mute. You are beauty amid desolation. You are not a victim; you are an answer. Imagine the power in this change of perspective."[1]

It is a thrilling time to be a Christian woman. Gender limitations from even thirty years ago are receding. Cultural divides are bridged as we speak. Opportunities available are infinite. International influence is entirely possible. Where we were once sidelined, we are now major contributors. Your gifts, talents, and passions can reach much further. You are more available than ever to God as a solution.

I believe He is knocking on the doors of His daughters in increasing intensity. At the beginning of time, creation had its first problem ("It is not good for the man to be alone" [Genesis 2:18]), and a woman was the answer. Now this planet suffers from countless injustices — poverty, unwanted children, broken families, addiction, disease, oppression, war, ecological decay, corruption, greed, famine, hopelessness — with a church that is silent on most of these, and women are still the answer.

You begin like Rahab did: Open the door. Recognize a movement of God when it's standing on your porch. Make the brave choice to align yourself with Christ's kingdom, even if you are all alone. The hurdles and solutions will come, but first you must tell God, "I'm in." This takes monumental courage, but *you are able*. As believers, we've been promised:

- You did not receive a spirit that makes you a slave again to fear, but you received the Spirit of sonship. And by him we cry, "*Abba*, Father." (Romans 8:15)
- God did not give us a spirit of timidity, but a spirit of power, of love and of self-discipline. (2 Timothy 1:7)
- Be strong and courageous. Do not be afraid or terrified because of them, for the LORD your God goes with you; he will never leave you nor forsake you. (Deuteronomy 31:6)
- On my servants, *both men and women*, I will pour out my Spirit in those days, and they will prophesy. (Acts 2:18, emphasis added)

These promises are terribly encouraging if you're willing to believe them. They eliminate the conspicuous obstructions delaying your buy-in. You are filled with a spirit of strength, guarded by a Savior who refuses to abandon you, and anointed by a Spirit who makes you capable of the impossible. I know it's true. I've seen it realized in too many women.

WHY I WANT RAHAB TO BE MY BEST FRIEND

Of course, the real adventure starts after you open the door. Then you realize what you signed on for. Once the spies were inside, Rahab's bravery was tested. No sooner did they enter than the king found out. He sent soldiers to bring the spies out of her house. Another knock.

"We know they're in there."

You know that white-hot adrenaline surge when you see flashing lights in your rearview mirror? How your legs get shaky and you're instantly sweaty? (I once got two tickets in three days. Speeding reform soon followed.) Imagine Rahab's fear with the soldiers on her porch demanding the spies *she was hiding on the roof.* My face would've betrayed me immediately, if I didn't retch on their shoes.

Yet our girl said calmly, "Yes, the men came to me, but I did not know where they had come from. At dusk, when it was time to close the city gate, the men left. I don't know which way they went. Go after them quickly. You may catch up with them." The first recorded instance of the old standby "They went thatta way."

What kind of woman defies a king, I ask you? What if they searched? What if they didn't believe her? What if they staked out her house and caught them leaving? The danger cannot be overstated. She risked her life, plain and simple, to protect two Hebrews preparing to conquer her city. Rahab was a fierce ally; God chose her well.

In the world of theological commentary, much is made of her lie here. Many find her deception undermining to her integrity. Politely, I say hogwash to that. Sometimes it is necessary to bear false witness to save our neighbor. She wouldn't sacrifice those she should protect, though saving them was contrary to the law. She was a feminine ancestor of other heroines who chose likewise, such as Harriet Tubman and the Underground Railroad and Corrie ten Boom's Jewish safe house during World War II.

History is replete with brave women who've risen up for justice. When I read of grandmothers in Africa raising fourteen grandchildren orphaned by AIDS, all alone, I am awestruck by their courage. Women are capable of impossible valor. Something is activated when life and love and honor are threatened. Even mild personalities transform under a godly directive for justice.

Many battles are reserved for men, as their spiritual design is more suited for conflict. But pity the fool who underestimates the warrior within a woman; you endanger her people or her passion, and she'll strike. Many enemies draw too near, dismissing a woman's fortitude, only to be leveled by her guts and determination. The victory does not always fall to the physically strong; we fight like girls, and enemies crumble before our unexpected weapons of love, wisdom, and bravery.

Satan realizes that women are formidable opponents — that's obvious from his attack against femininity from the beginning of creation. Besides outside oppression, it's a cunning strategy to tempt women to doubt their own courage. While the Devil keeps women sidelined with insecurity and complacency, every soul awaiting our intervention suffers — our children and husbands, the poor and oppressed, our local and international community. We are the answer to so many problems, sisters, yet scores are unwilling to fight.

Do you need to battle for your children? Lead the charge, brave mom. Perhaps it's for your marriage; don't you dare go down without fighting for reconciliation. Maybe God brought a war to your doorstep and you can't look away from poverty, violence, or abandonment.

Has He burdened you with another country? Maybe you're a foot soldier in the war against AIDS or malnutrition. Perhaps you've been selected for adopting a child; Jesus was obsessed with orphans. In your life, what injustice needs an ambassador for love, for healing?

When I dream of an entire generation attacking these challenges with their talents and passions, I nearly come unglued. With our intuition, gifts, capacity for compassion, and courage, there isn't a crisis that women could not solve. When we partner our skills with those of our men, God's dream of humanity working as one will be realized.

WHY I CAN'T DO IT: A DRAMA IN FOUR ACTS

Not that any of this is easy. If you've been around God for five minutes, you know better than that. Hiding the Hebrews was simple, but the obstacles followed: Rahab held off the soldiers with sheer guts, she had to get the spies out of town, plus the whole dilemma of staying alive under imminent attack if she weren't convicted of treason first.

No doubt the barriers facing your spiritual assignment are numerous. If the problem were easy, it would already be solved. Problems are problems because they're problematic. There are complications and red tape, hostility and suspicion. The timing is awkward, or resources are limited. There aren't enough hands on the issue, or there are too many with opposing perspectives. You've been given a no when you need a yes, or vice versa. The standard snags of fear and insecurity have you paralyzed. Plus, you have no idea what you're doing.

I feel you. Agreeing to write a book for God was like my wedding day, when everything was still lovely and happy. People gave us presents. There was dancing and cheese platters. People smiled as if to say, "Ahh, young love." (They were really thinking, *I give them four days until they have an official crisis over the toilet seat.*)

Come to find out, that first year or two was *hard*. Living with a man turned out to be a challenge. Developing the muscles of compromise and healthy communication was way more taxing than the editors at *Bride* magazine let on, what with their obsession with the wedding and zip on the subsequent marriage.

Most hurdles come after the metaphorical covenant is signed — I went from agreeing to write the book to contract in seven months — but I suffered through them. Learning to write a book, actually writing the words, juggling three kids under six, preparing for a writers' conference, figuring out what a book proposal was, defining my "pitch," consorting with real authors, preparing for rejection — terrifying, all.

I had a daily encounter that fall that went something like this:

Knock, knock.

Who's there?

It's me, your intestines. I've teamed up with your nervous stomach, and we'd like to meet you in the bathroom. Anxiety and fear of failure are meeting us in three minutes.

Admittedly, writing a book for a publisher's chopping block can hardly be compared with committing treason to save God's people. But still. It was the biggest assignment I'd received to date, only twenty-nine years old when that knock came. My obstacles? No time, no clue, no computer, three babies, no publishing history, no experience, no contacts, no agent.

"You will be rejected countless times," "All writers have their first book in a drawer somewhere unpublished," "All publishers hate writers and make it their mission to crush their esteem and extinguish their passion" (or something like that). This is what I read everywhere. It's what I heard from everyone. It was all true, if slightly embellished by the disgruntled. But at the risk of sounding trite, I'd received my orders, and I'm a rule follower on things like this. I assumed that if God was that clear, I better just do it and let Him worry over the impossibilities.

Faith is rather dumb like that.

RAHAB MAKES US ALL LOOK LIKE CHUMPS

Rahab told the spies, "The LORD your God is God in heaven above and on the earth below." We see the catalyst behind her bravery: a beautiful display of faith. Again, my experience pales in comparison. Since my career as a fetus, I've been exposed to every sermon, Bible study, conference, church service, worship team, curriculum, mission report, Christian book, speaker, and resource under the stars. If I *don't* believe God at this point, I am an idiot. The feats I've seen Him pull off cannot be numbered.

But all Rahab knew of God was how He miraculously protected this nomadic group, if you believed the rumors. She never met Him. She hadn't heard of His Law. She never saw His handiwork. No one in her community cared squat about Him. He was a complete mystery to her, except for the notable miracles surrounding His emerging reputation.

Yet the first person to declare God's sovereignty in the Promised Land was a Canaanite prostitute. She believed, barely knowing God's name. Not only that, she risked her life aligning with this God. The most primitive faith fueled one of the bravest moments in Scripture.

What possible excuse can we offer?

How many centuries must God prove His faithfulness until we believe it? How many wonders must we witness? How often do we need to read the 120-plus miracles in His Word? How many times must we see Jesus transform a life? A whole family? How regularly must His Spirit speak to us until we trust in His presence? How frequently must God deliver peace before we believe Him? With our exposure to all things God, if our faith is not developing, we will be without excuse one day.

I've had countless assignments since my foray into publishing, not the least of which is this gem: "You and Brandon start a church." As I write this, that's basically what we know. Hardly a detail is clear outside of that directive. This is the riskiest move we've ever taken. Nothing is guaranteed yet—not a salary, not success, not security, not support. As we stand on the cusp of obedience, we never have had so much at stake.

My usual inclination is to freak out. I'm a fretter. Failure and I have never gotten along, not to mention my high-maintenance desire to feed my children. This is uprooting our lives with no assurances. Yet panic has barely scratched at the door. In fact, my composure has spazzed hubby out. He's worried I'm having some sort of mental break or maybe quietly arranging an escape to abandon this train wreck.

I've just been here so many times with God. This moment is familiar. He has gently nudged me off the ledge so often, and, though free-falling a bit, I'm always caught by God's rescue net of faithfulness. This cycle has happened so frequently, I'm almost incapable of the old brand of fear. Certainly, there are concerns, but I can't *not* trust God. He's come through too many times.

I'm living the truth: "*You* will keep in perfect peace him whose mind is steadfast, because he trusts in you" (Isaiah 26:3, emphasis added). I am not calm on the outside and freak show on the inside. I'm not tanking up on sedatives to keep from going postal. Peace dipped down and overcame me in spite of myself. It is God's handiwork.

It's no mystery why women have such bravery; the Lord makes it possible. Fear is no match for the Spirit of peace. The more we go through this process with Him—assignment, obedience, deliverance—the deeper our courage develops. It goes like this with God:

1. It is impossible.
2. It is hard.
3. It is done.

Habitual faithfulness will change our lives, which will change the world. If God has called you to it, dear one, then it can be done.

THERE IS NO "I" IN "ALLY" (OR SOMETHING LIKE THAT)

Before letting them down by a rope through the city wall, Rahab asked for mercy. "Please swear to me by the LORD that you will show kindness to my family, because I have shown kindness to you." They told Rahab to hang a scarlet cord in her window and bring her entire family inside, and when they attached Jericho, they'd spare the people in the marked house. She then helped them escape, suggesting they hide in the hills for three days until the soldiers gave up the wild-goose chase she sent them on.

"Our lives for your lives!" promised the spies. God protects those who protect His people. Side with mercy, justice, and love and you'll ensure divine teamwork. As you evaluate your spiritual assignment, identify your allies. Perhaps, like Rahab, they are the very ones you're tasked with helping. How many mission workers say, "I went to serve them, but they served me"?

Shane Claiborne wrote of his friend Bob McIlvaine, whose son was killed on September 11, 2001. Bob not only believed that violence was not the answer but he sensed that the people of Iraq were dads, families, and children like we are. He and others who lost someone that sad day started a group called Families for Peaceful Tomorrows.

Their slogan is "Our grief is not a cry for war."

Many traveled to Iraq to comfort families who lost loved ones in this war. It was part of their spiritual assignment. Instead, "they share the stories of ordinary Iraqi people who would flood them with hugs and flowers and gifts to bring back to families who lost their loved ones in the September 11th attacks."[2] Encouragement often bubbles from the bottom up.

Who shares your passion? Who has been there already? Who can advise and encourage you? Who has the skills you lack for this task? Who shares your burden? Who is already on the ground? Who could be your prayer warrior? Who subscribes to this gospel? Who inspires you? Who is on the side of God's agenda?

Care about what Jesus cared about, collaborate with people who do too, and claim this promise:

> There is no wisdom, no insight, no plan
>   that can succeed against the LORD. (Proverbs 21:30)

It's a fairly straightforward strategy, ruined only by our self-absorption.

HAPPY EVER AFTER AND PASS THE KLEENEX

Our story ends well. When the walls of Jericho came down, Rahab and her family—identified by the red cord—were the only people spared. Everyone delivered on their promise: The spies protected her, and God brought His people into the Promised Land. Faith and courage compel God above most other sacrifices. Women are most dangerous to our Enemy when our belief convinces us to risk, and *God is for that girl.*

What of Rahab? It's easy to look on her red cord and see only a red flag. *Warning! Tainted goods! Stupid choices! Train wreck ahead!*

That is the tendency of believers yet to convert to the gospel of grace. Frankly, believing is easy; everyone is doing it. The citizens of Jericho believed too, but only Rahab had faith. Our gospel is not a safe one; it never has been. Faith is not for cowards.

As it always does, grace did more than save her life. Rahab became wife of Salmon, a prince of Israel. Her godliness is reflected in her exceptional son, Boaz — redeemer and husband of Ruth, great-grandfather of King David. Rahab and Ruth were only one generation apart, both named in the lineage of Christ. Theirs became a family of remarkable women.

In fact, in James's famous teaching on faith and action, he called but two witnesses from the collective history of God's people: Abraham — father of Israel, cornerstone of God's holy nation — and Rahab, daughter and warrior of the Most High. Everywhere else she is called "Rahab the prostitute" in Scripture, with one exception: When she is honored in Jesus' family tree in Matthew, she is called only "Rahab." That old distinction was removed under the grace of *El Shaddai*, who destroys the names over His daughters and overpowers the labels that defined us. Grace indeed deserves our praise since it does so much for its recipient. Grace does not smuggle women into heaven but raises us to heaven's requirements through faith and courage and the blood of Christ.

Dear one, embrace what grace can do for you; God withholds none of it. If He lifted you out of the depths of despair, there is more: He can set your feet on a rock. If on that rock you stand, He can put a new song in your mouth. If your heart already sings, He can establish your steps. If you have solid footing, He can commission the gospel to you. When He hands over the keys to His kingdom, there is no limit to your reach.

All the blessings of the covenant of mercy belong to you. If you have but a simple faith, you will yet comprehend how wide and long and high and deep is the love of Christ that removes our shame, develops our courage, and crowns us with honor.

Unfathomable is His grace.

Arise and enjoy it, daughter.

CHAPTER 6

Incongruent Segments

When You Don't Match the Church Ladies Who Wear Pantyhose

Myth #3:

God has a pecking order of favorites, centered on denomination and nationality.

RUTH 1

Jesus is suffering an identity crisis lately. Nowhere is this more apparent than in the vast array of (allegedly) Jesus-sanctioned products making their way into the Christian market. You've probably been assaulted by some, unfortunately. My girlfriend in the industry calls it "Jesus Junk."

Friends of mine hold a yearly contest to crown the reigning J.J. champ. Notable title holders include last year's dual finalists: praise panties (limited supply available) and Tickle Me Jesus (which I'm sure gave the Savior a nasty bout of nausea). The finest example was the memorable champ of 2005: "Ask Me Anything Jesus," a ten-inch, fuzzy, neon-pink Jesus with a Magic 8 Ball lodged in his gut. You could ask your burning question, shake the Messiah, and expect such answers as "I don't know—let me ask my dad" and "I died for this?" (Holy Spirit not included).

Honestly, I'm so embarrassed for Jesus. So many pimp Him out for profit, play on the ignorance of consumers, use His name to endorse every brand of tomfoolery, and publicly humiliate His honor. The exploitation of Jesus is beyond tragic; it cheapens the Cross and shames the church, and I suspect God won't tolerate it much longer.

So who is Jesus for? Whose side is He on? What exactly *does* He endorse? I've been challenged with this lately. Five years ago, I would've responded differently. Not that I have this sewn up, but I think it's not who Jesus is for, but who is for Him.

Again, God's Word is enlightening here. Perhaps this chapter will challenge what you've always believed about the Christian identity, particularly as a woman. I ask only that you remain open to the truth, whatever that is. Let's attempt to get on Jesus' side rather than making Him choose ours.

"YOU'RE GROUNDED" — GOD

Our brave heroine Rahab is the mother-in-law of the next beauty honored in the family tree of Jesus: Ruth. Let's see how she was grafted into this extraordinary family. Rahab was absorbed in the early stages of the Hebrew acquisition of the Promised Land. The Hebrews steadily conquered the groups who inhabited that holy region. In the time it took Rahab to get married, bear a son, and raise him to middle age, the Israelites entered a new season of their history.

The twelve tribes were established, inhabiting territory from the tribe of Simeon in the south to Dan in the north, spanning 150 miles. Rather than naming a king, God had them governed by judges, who were judicial and militaristic leaders. At best, this was Israel at her infancy. This was the Hebrews' first pass at establishment—their only history being 350 years as slaves, then forty years as homeless people. I tell you this because it helps me forgive the Israelites, as this period marks their most dismal years of failure and rebellion. This era lasted from 1350–1050 BC, roughly three hundred years of chronic disobedience.

I liken these to the teenage years of Israel. The Hebrews were beyond the totally dependent baby phase, when God literally kept them alive with manna from heaven and water from rocks. They weren't yet to the stage of spiritual responsibility, ready to receive the Messiah and launch His church. They were in that adolescent phase, when God's parenting was totally getting on their nerves, and He didn't even understand them, and His rules were so lame. *Gosh!*

They'd push the envelope, get busted, get grounded, fly right for a while, and then do it again. Pick any page recording these years, and the Hebrews were either griping about God's standards, wishing they had a different dad, or bawling their eyes out, begging Him to rescue them from the mess they'd gotten into.

This is important to this chapter, because God was obsessed with protecting the Israelites from the idolatry of their pagan neighbors. God did what any concerned parent does with rebellious teens: He fanatically monitored their friendships and put strict limits on who they hung with. No going out with the bad kids, if you will. ("I don't care what their parents let them do; I haven't raised you to act like derelicts.") He said things like:

- "You must not do as they do in the land of Canaan, where I am bringing you. Do not follow their practices." (Leviticus 18:3)
- "Do not place a foreigner over you, one who is not a brother Israelite." (Deuteronomy 17:15)

- "You shall not make a covenant with the people of this land."
  (Judges 2:2)
- "Do not worship the gods of the Amorites, in whose land you
  live" (Judges 6:10)

This talk went on and on. This was God's attempt to develop a
holy nation. Basically, He created steep boundaries between who was
in (the Israelites) and who was out (everyone else). God stamped His
endorsement on the Hebrews, raised His banner over their territories,
and positioned Himself against their enemies.

GOD BLESS THE USA

This is precisely how many Christian Americans describe His covenant
with us, too. America is God's turf, right? JesUSAves, or so I read on
a bumper sticker. "Many of us American evangelicals not only make
Jesus into an American," wrote Tony Campolo in *Speaking My Mind*,
"but also view Him as a deity who provides sanctification for our afflu-
ent, consumeristic lifestyle. We have created a Jesus who will fight to
preserve America and all that our nation stands for." In a speech to
the National Religious Broadcasters in 2003, President Bush received
a standing ovation after declaring the war in Iraq a cause defined by
religious absolutes. He said that our nation sought no selfish gain in
this war and that "we were on the side of God."

Says who? Jesus?

When He said, "Love your enemies"? Or when He said, "Those
who live by the sword will die by the sword"? The Prince of Peace
grieves no less for the loss of innocents in Iraq than for those covered
in the stars and stripes. If it's His endorsement we seek, then it must
be His example we follow, for He didn't conquer an oppressive Roman
regime with violence but overcame the world through love.

This pro-American God rhetoric is so pervasive, it feels radical to challenge it. But, girls, can we honestly believe we are the prototype for a modern-day holy nation? America accurately represents the holiness of Christ about as much as the Jesus Junk I referenced. Even if we were a nation of model believers, God doesn't throw His lot in with a people based on political or geographical or national boundaries anymore.

"Rebirth [through salvation in Christ] means that we have a new paradigm of 'us' and 'them.' Our central identity is no longer biological," wrote Shane Claiborne. "And our central allegiance is no longer national. Our pronouns change. Our new 'us,' as Jesus teaches, is the church, the people of God doing the will of the Father."[2] We have brothers and sisters in nearly every nation, and God's supernatural work in other countries is beyond extraordinary.

God's allegiance belongs to the believer who trusts in Him, regardless of (or in spite of) nationality, skin color, traditions, political affiliation, denomination, or birthright. We are on dangerous ground when we assume He is on our side, carte blanche. Is patriotism wrong? Certainly not. But as believers we must resist the tendency to say, "My country right or wrong, but right or wrong, my country!" Our new citizenship is in heaven, and God transcends all nations. Our prayer should be, as Tony Campolo suggested, "My country—may she always be right. And when she is not right, may I do my best to call my country to repentance."[3]

No nation, no group, no denomination, and no human can act contrary to God's Word and His will and expect His approval. He is not defined by our boundaries. He never has been. No one owns the rights to God's blessings. He will bless the heart that belongs to Him and reject those who use His name for a heavenly endorsement. Period.

God is not American.

Nor is He Republican.

Not even Southern Baptist (sorry, Dad).

FORMULAS ARE FOR ALGEBRA

The temptation is to figure God all out, make alliterative lists about Him (God loves *light*, *lambs*, and *long walks in the park*), and declare the market identified and cornered, when, in fact, God is totally surprising most of the time. About the moment you categorize Him, He'll wreck your formula.

My friends *think* they have me figured out, too, which I don't care for, as I've mentioned. So sometimes I mess with them. For example, I'm not very girly in the traditional sense. I don't care for fluff and fuss. I'm no-clutter, no-frills.

I've led Bible study for years, and it's hilarious to compare mine to others going on in our church or community. The other girly leaders make fancy name tags with ribbons and calligraphy. Their study packets are printed on beautiful paper with trim, all bound with silk bows or some such. They set up welcome tables with flower arrangements and thematic decorations. Each woman gets some cute favor that matches the theme, and everyone goes home feeling precious.

I have the feminine sensitivity of a twelve-year-old boy.

My girls get a reading syllabus on white computer paper, we don't have name tags unless my small-group leaders bring them, and their take-home favor is homework. Snacks? Themes? Thoughtfulness? What is this, kindergarten? I assume everyone is there for the same reason I am: They are crazy obsessed with God's Word and can't wait to spend hours studying maps, commentaries, and time lines.

So one semester, I decided to surprise my girls with some display of girlishness on our first night of Bible study. I realize it won't wow you, but in Jen terms, I went all out: Their syllabus was on pink paper in

Kristen font, and I printed our theme verse on cute bordered card stock. There. Everyone happy?

I started passing out my art projects/handouts, and—wait for it—the reaction began immediately:

"What is this?!"
"Who did this for you?"
"What's going on?"
"I'm scared."

I was quite pleased with myself, even after admitting that since I didn't own a hole punch, I ran a power drill through the stack of verse cards so they could tie them onto their journals. (My arts-and-crafts savvy is fairly limited.)

MOAB SHMOAB

In our story, God pulled out the proverbial cute bordered card stock instead of white computer paper as usual. Rahab's family, including her grown son, Boaz, lived in Bethlehem, where they built a lovely Hebrew life. They owned a great deal of land, employed a large staff, and were well respected in the community. Boaz followed all the biblical rules of governing his estate, and everything up till now was, well, white computer paper.

Before we meet Miss Cute Bordered Card Stock, understand something about Moab, Israel's pagan neighbor to the east. These two regions had a hostile history. Evidently, Moab didn't care for Israel's killing their citizens and conquering their land. It didn't set well. The pages of Scripture are filled with their bloody confrontations. Israel couldn't stand the idols Moab tempted them with (except when they were totally worshipping them). Because of following the god Chemosh, any Moabite or his sons to the tenth generation were forbidden to enter the assembly of the Lord (see Deuteronomy 23:3). In fact, God said, "Moab is my washbasin" (Psalm 60:8), a place to wash His dusty feet.

So when a famine hit Bethlehem, most Hebrews stayed put rather than cohabitate with the despised Moabites a few miles east. Remember, God was terribly firm on this boundary. But this one family, relatives of Boaz, took their chances in godless Moab rather than starve in Judah. So Elimelech and Naomi, along with their two sons, moved to Moab and merged their lives with the enemy.

In the first five verses of Ruth, Elimelech died, Naomi's sons married Moabite women — Ruth and Orpah — then the sons died, leaving three childless widows. Here I'd like to pause and acknowledge the tenderness of God (stay with me). That we even have this story is a credit to His affection for women. In patriarchal days, the devastation these girls faced was just part of being a woman. No husbands, no children, meant no worth. This story should've just gone away, another forgotten feminine tragedy.

Yet here we see this hopeless pseudo-family of women attract the eye of God. Why? They had no prestige, wealth, spiritual significance, honor, or even righteousness. Naomi breached God's holy boundaries at the first sign of trouble, and Ruth and Orpah were foreign idolaters. But although Boaz turned out to be quite the hero, this book is titled "Ruth."

Friend, you are loved by a God who attends to brokenness. If you're alone or estranged from God's family, even by your choosing, nothing can obscure you from Christ's attention. If the whole world moves on while you are stuck, you aren't alone. Like these women, maybe your best titles were stripped: *wife*, maybe *mother*, and life seems over. But no loss, no sin, no heartache removes your title as daughter of the Almighty.

Once God had indeed "come to the aid of his people by providing food for them," Naomi decided to go home. She urged her daughters-in-law to stay in Moab with good reason: They could still remarry, their fathers could provide until then, and better in Moab than despised in Judah. If those girls had any sense of self-preservation, they should've agreed. Only one did.

SALVATION ≠ WALKING AN AISLE AND PRAYING WITH A DEACON

So we finally see what Ruth is made of. Jeopardizing her future, she refused to leave Naomi. She clung to her with these now famous words: "Don't urge me to leave you or to turn back from you. Where you go I will go, and where you stay I will stay. Your people will be my people and your God my God. Where you die I will die, and there I will be buried. May the LORD deal with me, be it ever so severely, if anything but death separates you and me."

I love her.

They were greeted with surprise in Bethlehem because Naomi left ten years ago, presumed dead or lost I'm sure. Plus, she returned not with husband or sons but with "Ruth the Moabitess," reminding me how Boaz's mother was once "Rahab the prostitute." The white-computer-paper types disqualify one for her sin and the other for her heritage.

Wouldn't we, too? How would Ruth be perceived in America today? Detained because she spoke Arabic? Flagged as a possible terrorist? Ripped from Naomi's arms for questioning or just looked on with suspicion? We'd pass instant judgment on her beliefs, ignorant of her sincere faith confession.

How quickly we judge other cultures and faith systems. As if Jesus was born in Dallas or something. Can we possibly claim to know how God draws mankind in? At the conception of His community, God told Abraham, "Through your offspring *all nations* on earth will be blessed" (Genesis 22:18, emphasis added). The nations are referenced almost two hundred times in Scripture. Are we arrogant enough to assume He draws people only through religious models *we've* established? What are we, 250 years old as a nation? That much time passes in two paragraphs in Scripture. We did not write the book on God.

You won't find a typical suburban megachurch on the street corners of most nations on this planet. God has many weapons of intimacy, and only a fool limits His reach. Scripture tells us that He draws mankind through creation, His Spirit (whom no human can fully understand), the love of people, a sense of eternity, and justice. I refuse to quantify God's methods or scope. Jesus is the way, but we can't determine who has genuinely encountered the resurrected Jesus and who hasn't.

Jesus said that two groups will be surprised when this life is over: those who flaunt their self-righteous merits only to hear, "I never really knew you," and those who will be welcomed into heaven asking, "Lord, when did we ever love You?" and He'll reply, "Whatever you did for the least and lost people, you did for Me" (see Matthew 25:31-41). The incarnation of Christ is divinely activated and divinely discerned.

Paul reminded us, "Who are you to judge someone else's servant? To his own master he stands or falls. And he will stand, for the Lord is able to make him stand" (Romans 14:4). Believers, may we never show contempt for God's mercy by restricting it to a Western experience.

"WE WILL PRAISE AND LIFT YOU HIGH, EL SHADDAI"

As women graft into the family of God, this issue of acceptable stock must be addressed. The mainstream evangelical model boils it down to this: conservative, Republican, pro-war, anti-gay, traditional domestic roles, Amy Grant, toe the party line.

Jesus' church members have always preferred exclusivity. Then: Keep out the Gentiles, keep out the uncircumcised, keep out the skeptics. Now: Keep out the homosexuals, keep out the prostitutes, keep out the *sinners*. I can't square this with Jesus' ideas, like how His church is a hospital for the sick and a sanctuary for offenders. Or when He said that the greatest display of our faith is how we love people.

Loving people isn't the same as condoning sin. Welcoming into your church a stripper who hasn't yet quit her job isn't endorsing her career choice. (Ditto homosexuals.) It's saying, "Look, this church is full of people with sin habits, some of which we know about and others successfully kept secret from everyone else. If there are two hundred of us in this room, someone here is hooked on porn, a few are poisonous gossips, somebody is being eaten alive by hatred toward whomever, somebody's having sex outside marriage, quite a few wish they could, several of us are in the grip of envy, and so on. The church is packed with sinners, and the stripper isn't worse. What we care about is that the sinners here are in the process of letting Jesus forgive them and clean up their lives."

The Pharisees constantly tried to pin Jesus down on issues and political positions. Everyone wanted Him to declare a side, endorse the status quo, but He wouldn't do it:

"Why don't you fast?"

"Why do you work on the Sabbath?"

"Why don't you wash your hands before you eat?"

"Taxes should go to Caesar or not?"

"How can you eat with sinners?"

"Who is my 'neighbor'?"

"Should we worship on this mountain or that mountain?"

"You agree with the law on stoning this adulterous
    woman, right?"

Geography, pedigree, and issues have always mattered more to people than to God. Even Jesus was disqualified by the pious: "A prophet does not come out of Galilee" (John 7:52). With Jesus' affinity for the misunderstood, mistreated, and misfits, He and His friends would be welcome in very few churches today. If Jesus had a prototype for His followers crafted around issues, He would've described it. Do we think He forgot to address these human conventions that divide us?

If God selected a Moabite woman for the lineage of His Son *in a time when the boundaries were totally rigid*, who am I to sit as a sterner judge after Jesus destroyed those boundaries? "All of you who were baptized into Christ have clothed yourselves with Christ. There is neither Jew nor Greek, slave nor free, male nor female, for you are all one in Christ Jesus. If you belong to Christ, then you are Abraham's seed, and heirs according to the promise" (Galatians 3:27-29).

THE DEVIL WEARS PANTYHOSE

The arrogance of the church wounds many women who come to it unconventionally. As tragic as a prefabricated model of womanhood is, it's worse when newcomers are shamed into mimicking it. Women are unique offenders here and often act like fierce guard dogs, protecting the Image with saccharine smiles and condescending comments.

My Girlfriend Steph served in a small church with her husband after college. It was a zillion years old in this teeny town, and here came two fresh-faced ministers, thrilled to lead the students there. After a couple of Sundays, the "church ladies" pulled her aside and helped her understand this basic doctrine of God's worldwide church: "It is terribly inappropriate for you not to wear pantyhose."

Have mercy.

As if God gives a hollerin' hoot about nylons.

After moving to our church in Austin, Steph asked me, "Why

don't the women wear pantyhose here?" My simple answer: "Because they were created by Satan, obviously. But if you'd like to bind your crotch with demonic fabric and squeeze your cheeks into a unibutt, I'm sure our stores sell them."

Girls, pantyhose or jeans, heels or flip-flops, tattoos or pearls, simple hoops or multiple piercings, Southern Baptist or Catholic, Republican or Democrat, black or white, American or not . . . WHO CARES?! What difference do these distinctions make in God's holy family? Do these affect the way we love others? Do they change the study of Scripture? Do they alter the beauty of the gospel? Jesus transcends every preference, every heritage, every nation.

Through our diversity, Jesus has skin in the game everywhere. He anoints ambassadors in violent urban areas, tidy suburbs, artistic communities, different political parties, at the top of the executive world, at the bottom of the service industry, within the passionate young, the experienced aged, the traditional, the unconventional, Americans, Europeans, Iraqis, anyone, everywhere. He will be glorified in the nations, not just on Sunday mornings in suburban churches by men in suits and women in pantyhose.

PEACE IN THE MIDDLE EAST (AND IN THE CHURCH LOBBY)

Daughter, maybe you came from a Moab. Maybe you're a Moabitess, judged because your pedigree doesn't match the white-computer-paper version in Bethlehem. Receive this today: You are a sister of Ruth, favored by God, made perfect by a perfect Savior. God has never been swayed by convention, even if He once established it.

If you feel like the black sheep in God's family, you are in good company. With almost no exceptions, women in Scripture were too. They came from the wrong lands, the wrong families, the wrong tribes. God made His position clear: His servants are qualified by their strength, their faith, their courage. The only image He requires of us, girls, is His—the image we bear as His daughters.

We reflect it so beautifully.

Maybe He's calling you out of Moab to the abundance of His land, like Ruth. Or maybe you are to remain in your Moab and be the hands of Christ there. You might be the most effective cute bordered card stock ever known. But the church of Jesus must reject the dividing lines when He shed His blood to eliminate those barriers.

The Naomis of Bethlehem should protect the Ruths of Moab; the sisters of Ruth should respect the Naomis they encounter. There's no Bethlehem, no Moab, no borders in the family of Christ. It is not ours to shut doors, but to throw them open and welcome the beloved of God.

You've been designed like you are. You were born where you were born intentionally. Your background is the foundation God chose for you. You have a traditional or nontraditional bent on purpose. Your race was planned. The culture you grew up in shaped you into the Christ follower He needed you to be.

Stop pushing against your heritage. Stop fighting against someone else's. God needs daughters of every race, creed, tradition, and nation. He selected you, perfectly understanding where you came from and where you're going. He chose other women precisely because of their trajectory. Neither geography nor heritage matter—neither American nor Afghani, neither traditional nor radical, neither Baptist nor Catholic, neither preacher's daughter nor atheist's daughter, neither baptized in a church nor dunked in a river . . .

> Neither circumcision nor uncircumcision means anything; what counts is a new creation. Peace and mercy to all who follow this rule, even to the Israel of God. (Galatians 6:15-16)

CHAPTER 7

Feminine Dimensions

When the Lantern Is Hanging Firmly Inside, Girl, Paint the House!

Truth #3:

Women are beautiful.

RUTH 2–4

My family has a long and distinguished history of vanity. Our matriarch of the "more is more" theory is my ninety-one-year-old grandma. Nearly all her body has revolted against her razor-sharp mind, which she is irritated to the high heavens about, but it hasn't slowed down her pursuit of beauty.

When Grandma moved into an assisted-living facility last year, she immediately sized up her competition. Word on the street was that Lucille was known for her sassy flair. It was common knowledge at Beckett Meadows. Rumor was she won the Christmas-door-decorating contest two of the last three years, what with her good taste and all. According to Hazel and some of the other old girls, Lucille was the senior version of America's Next Top Model.

Guess who was Grandma's tablemate in the dining room?

Near Christmas, I was eating lunch with Grandma when Lucille showed up wearing a red feather boa and Santa necklace with blinking lights. She sauntered in like a geriatric Mae West. I acted nice, of course ("Oh, Lucille, aren't you sparkly today!"), but she had thrown down the gauntlet. It was on.

"Grandma, you need to step up your game!" I said to her, even though she'd only been there a week or two. "Lucille has no idea who she's up against. She has not begun to see you in all your glory. She *owns* you right now, Grandma! You need to start bringing it!"

Don't think my Grandma doesn't park her wheelchair every week at the nail salon to get her Carmelo Soprano acrylics filled. Rings on six fingers? Check. Coordinating separates from Chadwick's, Chico's, and/or JCPenney catalog? Every day. If her hair isn't right or her beauty regimen is hindered, she takes her meal in her room, thank you. She doesn't want Lucille's big old head to explode with superiority.

She's even been specific about her burial clothes (black silk suit with sequined lapels) lest we deliver her to the arms of Jesus in yesterday's fashion. Grandma might suffer from cracked vertebrae, blocked arteries, strokes, and osteoporosis, but she looks good.

And all God's women said, "Amen."

Women and beauty: an ancient, divine combination.

PRETTY WOMAN, WALKING DOWN THE STREET (THE KIND I'D LIKE TO MEET)

Huuuuuhhh (that's me sighing). This topic could easily take up the entire book. How has this gotten so messed up? Girls, we've been blessed with the equivalent of a financial windfall. It's powerful. It draws in friend and enemy. It is wielded in wisdom or foolishness. It compels some to wonderment and others to exploitation. It is an agent of healing or a tool for destruction. Men have stormed gates for the love of it and locked down in fear of it. It's been misunderstood since the garden.

It is our beauty, and hardly a more divine gift exists.

"God has given this Beauty to Eve, to every woman," wrote John and Stasi Eldredge in *Captivating*. "Beauty is core to a woman—who she is and what she longs to be—and one of the most glorious ways we bear the image of God in a broken and often ugly world. . . . It is an essence every woman carries from the moment of her creation."[1]

Men and women display God's character uniquely. I love so many things about men that I adore in my heavenly Father: their strength, their desire to protect, their courage, their masculinity. A man is so like God when he leads in integrity. Their sense of adventure, their penchant for risk taking—all good, good, good. When I observe the gifts men offer, I am stunned by their Creator.

But as much as I applaud men, I'm more in awe about how God fashioned women. We reflect the parts of Him that heal and nourish, the beauty that invites the world to rest in it. Women reveal His glory most dramatically. Jean Anouilh said, "Beauty is one of the rare things that do not lead to doubt of God."[2] Indeed.

A woman was the grand finale of creation, God's crowning masterpiece. Every element of creation swelled, a crescendo of beauty: light, oceans, forests, stars, animals, man—"It is not good for the man to be alone"—*woman*. I imagine that all sounds quieted, all motions ceased, creation respectfully bowed in awe of her. She was not an afterthought or accessory to Adam; she was the crowning jewel of God's hands. He said of her, "*For this reason* a man will leave his father and mother and be united to his wife" (Genesis 2:24, emphasis added).

For this reason, men will go to war. For this reason, laughter will triumph over mourning. For this reason, art is inspired and executed. For this reason, hope lives. For this reason, broken hearts are healed.

For this reason, we have music and plays and literature and paintings and children and grace and charm and loveliness and beauty and God's own glory.

For this reason: woman.

It's no wonder beauty has been distorted. The Enemy brings his strongest attacks on what threatens him most. With such powerful potential, he'll do anything to destroy the reflection of Christ. To keep them from just being beautiful, he pressures women to become manipulative, ashamed, obsessed, careless. He lures men to become not respectful but fearful, abusive, judgmental, lustful. All of these are dangers of mishandled beauty.

I'LL BE THERE FOR YOU (THESE FIVE WORDS I SWEAR TO YOU)

Again, I'm grateful for the Word. Let's see how Ruth handled this gift. Ruth means "lovely friend" or "beautiful." Indeed, her life brought integrity to her name. She was entirely beautiful and attracted the townspeople, the workers, the foreman, Boaz, the elders, the women, even the eye of God.

She had no conventional merits; she was a widowed, childless, foreign Moabite without a penny, a man, a child, a home. But how many women have every traditional possession and position but lack any semblance of beauty? Our glory doesn't come from outward adornment, be it physical or circumstantial. Our beauty is patterned after God's; our visual beauty is a reflection of character. A God who created rivers and mountains and wildflowers is a God I must know. His beauty is indicative of His nature, as is ours.

Ruth's beauty was demonstrated in her allegiance to Naomi, refusing to leave against her own best interests. Let's pause and acknowledge her loyalty. What a forerunner we have in her. How beautiful is the woman who walks through the valley of shadow with another. There is much glory in her courage and devotion.

Women are particularly beautiful in this area. Cross a woman's child and find out yourself. Insult her husband and be prepared to go fisticuffs. Injure her girlfriend and I fear for your life. Exploit the innocent; there'll be hell to pay. Women are faithful, beautifully so. Women historically put their needs aside to give another the gift of their presence.

You can count on a woman.

Do you see how this beautifies the earth? It alleviates fear that plagues so many. Men are drawn to its safety as well as its nobility. When the whole earth leaves or betrays or neglects or doubts, women stay. They are a soft place to fall, a given. Their loyalty has given many men the courage to face their giants, the inspiration to rise up. If every man, child, and friend had a woman who believed in them, can you imagine how they'd be released into their destinies?

LUCK BE A LADY TONIGHT

Ruth's faithfulness to Naomi was the seed that grew into her redemption. Back in Bethlehem, poor and homeless, Ruth again delivered: "Let me go to the fields and pick up the leftover grain behind anyone in whose eyes I find favor." In ancient Israel, landowners were required to leave what the harvesters missed so the poor, the alien, the widow, and the fatherless could glean for their needs.

Scripture tells us, "As it turned out, [Ruth] found herself working in a field belonging to Boaz, who was from the clan of Elimelech." I love this lingo. Randomly, luckily, by chance, as it turned out, strangely, coincidentally, she found herself—these are not phrases recognized in the heavens. There is no *random* with God, though sometimes His sovereignty is veiled.

It's like my kids' Christmas gifts. Brandon takes our kids to the dollar store to purchase presents each year. We anticipate the fruits of this excursion more than any holiday wonder. Upon first glance, their choices seem, well, a little random:

- A plug-in, light-up Jesus for my mom (a possible Jesus Junk contender)
- A coffee mug for me that says, "Kiss, Kiss, Kiss, Still No Prince"
- A bracelet that read, "A Mother's Love," for my unwed sister with no children
- A pair of pom-poms for my twenty-seven-year-old sister
- Nose-hair trimmers for my dad

These are opened under the ecstatic gaze of our children, who barely contain their anticipation. When we're too slow, they rip the paper off themselves so we get to our treasures quicker. They search our faces, positive our lives will be changed by their gifts. Come to find out, they only *seem* random, when in fact every one has an explanation:

- Grana gets up early, so she needs to see in the dark. Plus, she likes Jesus.
- You *haven't* found a prince, Mom. You married Dad.
- Aunt Lindsay has "a mother," and she has "love" — duh.
- Aunt Cortney is so cheerful. Those are to shake when she's happy.
- Pepaw has fur in his nose.

So, you see, these gifts aren't random at all. They are deliberate, thought-out. Only a fool can't see that. You might think they grabbed the first light-up Jesus they saw, but you'd be wrong. Ask

Brandon — who endured the dollar store for three hours only to spend sixteen dollars — whether these were hasty, random purchases (bless him).

So it is with God. He moves intentionally, guiding us to the right fields with the right people at the right time, though we may not recognize it initially. On Ruth's first day in Boaz's field, he spotted her. "Whose young woman is that?" he asked his foreman. If his eye was drawn to her physical beauty, he was about to be floored by her inner beauty.

SHE WORKS HARD FOR THE MONEY, SO YOU BETTER TREAT HER RIGHT

The foreman replied, "She is the Moabitess who came back from Moab with Naomi. She said, 'Please let me glean and gather among the sheaves behind the harvesters.' She went into the field and has worked steadily from morning till now, except for a short rest in the shelter."

With that, Boaz was in love.

Do you see the power of beauty? It invites, it inspires, it makes a man crazy. There is nothing a man won't do for a beautiful woman, one of integrity and kindness. Boaz's heart nearly leapt out of his chest. Gorgeous, compassionate, strong work ethic, humble, loyal Ruth — he fell all over himself to protect her. This is what beauty does to the heart of a man.

He made a beeline for Ruth. "Stay here with my servant girls. Watch the field where the men are harvesting, and follow along after the girls. I have told the men not to touch you. And whenever you are thirsty, go and get a drink from the water jars the men have filled."

At this, she bowed down with her face to the ground. She exclaimed, "Why have I found such favor in your eyes that you notice me — a foreigner?"

Boaz replied, "I've been told all about what you have done for your

mother-in-law since the death of your husband—how you left your
father and mother and your homeland and came to live with a people
you did not know before. May the LORD repay you for what you have
done. May you be richly rewarded by the LORD, the God of Israel,
under whose wings you have come to take refuge."

Completely enamored, Boaz made sure she had dinner (staying
just to keep an eye on things, I'm sure). The second she left, he told his
workers to leave extra grain for her, and for Pete's sake, don't embarrass
her! Be nice to her! Don't say one mean thing! I'm sure he watched her
the rest of the day, probably didn't get a wink of sleep that night.

God love him.

Girls, don't let the stereotype of the brutish, oblivious male fool
you. Nothing evokes tenderness in a man like a beautiful woman. Look
at the songs they write, the books they author, the movies they make,
the lengths they go to secure the object of their affection. No, men are
not insensitive; they sometimes act that way to mask their vulnerability, because a beautiful woman makes them tremble. She makes him
lose his mind with affection and desire.

SHOT THROUGH THE HEART AND YOU'RE TO BLAME
(YOU GIVE LOVE A BAD NAME)

Notice what drew Boaz, what has always drawn man to woman. It
was the beauty of Ruth's feminine heart—vulnerable, humble, but
still courageous and faithful. Her tenderness was untainted by her
circumstances. "Masculine women cause men to dig in their heels
and fight for their position," wrote Michelle McKinney Hammond.
"If women rediscovered the art and the power of their own femininity, thus releasing men to be the men they were created to be, these
negative acts of affirming their identity as men—through abuse and
intimidation—would no longer be an option."[3]

This is where our beauty gets veiled, not in the five pounds we gain or the skin we inherited. It's when women lose their softness and refuse to be vulnerable. When we strive and clamor and claw our way up, men go on the defensive. What if Ruth stormed Boaz and commanded some protection? What if she threw his responsibility in his face, demanding her rights? If she barked at the servants or flaunted her sexuality to the workers, Ruth's story would be entirely different.

Sometimes the men in our lives don't fight for us because we haven't given them any reason to. We've traded in beauty for control, and it's ugly. Don't misunderstand me; I'm not asking you to be a helpless, hapless beauty in distress. That is simply another way to manipulate men. There is no honor in that.

But to be tender, available, honest—this draws a real man. Ruth conducted herself neither as the seductress or the victim, and Boaz nearly had a coronary trying to get to her. God designed us this way. As much as beauty is mystical, it is also practical; every woman has it, and no man can resist it. God is brilliant. The essence of a woman activates the design of a man. The best in a man is brought out by the best in a woman.

Every time.

Naomi saw this the second Ruth walked in, arms full of "extra" grain, a flush in her cheeks, a smile on her lips. "Where did you glean today? Where did you work? Blessed be *the man* who took notice of you!"

I'll say.

THE ANCIENT GOSPEL OF REBA

This arrangement continued until the end of the harvest, when Naomi stepped up Ruth's game. Because Boaz was family (a relative on Naomi's late husband's side), Ruth had not only Boaz's favor but the law in her corner. This was Naomi's ace: The closest relative must marry Ruth, since her husband died and left her childless. This ensured her protection and continuance of the family line.

Naomi knew what to do: "My daughter, should I not try to find a home for you, where you will be well provided for? Is not Boaz, with whose servant girls you have been, a kinsman of ours? Tonight he will be winnowing barley on the threshing floor. Wash and perfume yourself, and put on your best clothes. Then go down to the threshing floor, but don't let him know you are there until he has finished eating and drinking. When he lies down, note the place where he is lying. Then go and uncover his feet and lie down. He will tell you what to do."

What the heck? An explanation is offered by the great theologian Reba McEntire: "Here's your one chance, Fancy, don't let me down. Forgive me for what I do, but if you want out, well, it's up to you. Now don't let me down, hon, your mama's gonna move you uptown." Or something like that. This was the biblical version of Mama washin' and combin' and curlin' Ruth's hair, and paintin' her eyes and lips (then she stepped into a satin dancin' dress that had a split on the side clean up to her hip). Sorry. I'm having a hard time stopping.

Mama was moving Ruth uptown, straight up. And guess what, dear ones? She didn't advise Ruth to showcase that loyalty or work ethic Boaz was already captivated by. No advice 'bout asking for help or acting just a teeny pathetic. Uh-uh. No, it was game time.

BAM! Boaz never had a chance.

I don't know how your man acted when you dolled yourself up and laid on his feet after he'd had a bit to drink, but this totally worked for Ruth. Evidently, the ancient equivalent of a marriage proposal was Ruth asking Boaz to "spread the corner of your garment over me." This was aided by the smell of perfume and the beauty of her wardrobe, of course. Long hair, young glow, smelled like an angel—I bet Boaz lost consciousness.

MY DARLING, YOU LOOK WONDERFUL TONIGHT

Physical beauty has gotten bad press. Anything so supremely wonderful is bound to. I hardly want to waste time discussing the narrow parameters of beauty. Don't we know this, girls? Does anyone look at a ninety-five-pound, sixteen-year-old model as a worthy prototype? If those images once made me insecure, now they just make me sad. (Poor girls. They look so hungry. Eat a sandwich!) Women have staged a mutiny against the pursuit of unattainable, unrealistic beauty, and, frankly, the rest of the world doesn't suffer this issue the way the West does. Physical beauty comes in every size, shape, and color. Women are beautiful in their glorious diversity. The end.

However, resisting the siren song of vapid beauty, many Christian women declared any version of it godless, vain, superficial. As if God didn't create woman as the most breathtaking, awe-inspiring vision on the planet! Guess what? A woman *is* beautiful. Deal with it. Your hair, the curves of your body, your bone structure, the sound of your voice, gentle hands, the color of your cheeks, your eyelashes, your form — God outdid Himself.

Solomon told his bride, "Show me your face, let me hear your voice; for your voice is sweet and your face is lovely" (2:14). Ralph Ellison wrote of a woman, "Had the price of looking been blindness, I would have looked."[4] Emerson wrote, "If eyes were made for seeing, then Beauty is its own excuse for being."[5] "Women are always beautiful," wrote Ville Valo.[6] The beauty of women is a gift bestowed on humanity. It is a great and glorious good, and the whole world needs it.

God created women like the oceans and mountains and all that screams His name with external beauty. Would we shame the rivers for being too lovely? Judge the stars as superficial? Are the wildflowers simply vain? Should we chastise the rain forests for showing off?

John F. Kennedy said, "I look forward to an America which will not be afraid of grace or beauty."[7]

I TAKE TWO STEPS FORWARD, I TAKE TWO STEPS BACK

I, for one, am a fan. I like a little makeup and a good pair of jeans. I spent more than I'll admit on a good hair straightener. My Girlfriend Karen told me, "Hey, when the lantern is hanging firmly inside, girl, paint the house!"

Yet repeatedly, women confess to me a version of this statement: "I don't trust any woman who looks like she spent more than ten minutes getting ready. I'm looking for depth, not vanity."

This hurts me every time I hear it. Girlfriends, this is just another version of the stupid beauty game. Passing judgment on a woman by how she looks is foolish, regardless of which direction the judgment goes. Just like it's ridiculous to disqualify a woman because she's not pretty (thin, tall, leggy, young, sexy, voluptuous, and/or hot) enough, it is equally unfair to assume that caring how you look indicates a shallow heart or dubious motives.

Isn't that one way Christian men have mishandled beauty? During Jesus' day, the rabbis heaped scorn on Eve, claiming the serpent had sex with her and this "infused her with lust." Contrary to Scripture, many taught that women were more prone to sin than men. "For evil are women, my children . . . the angel of the Lord told me, and taught me, that women are overcome by the spirit of fornication more than men." And, "If one gazes at the little finger of a woman, it is as if he gazed at her secret place!" Women were held accountable for the lust of men.[8] If I have a drinking problem, it's not fair to blame wine for being delicious and rich and scrumptious with cheese. God made the wine that way. Perhaps my tendency toward excess and drunkenness is the issue. Sin can ruin any perfect gift (see: sex, spiritual gifts, marriage, motherhood, authority, the church, influence, wealth, freedom, and so on.) When we decide that beauty is the problem, we malign ourselves with God's very nature.

Daughter, you are beautiful, inwardly and outwardly. That is not up for debate any more than we could argue whether a sunset is lovely or not. Beauty has given women trouble forever, but not because it is ungodly. On the contrary, it's the godliest characteristic we bear.

Anything as powerful as beauty will be exploited or suffocated. It is exploited by men who fail to protect the beauty of women. It's exploited by women who use it as a weapon, a bargaining chip. It has certainly been suffocated by the church, who equated beauty with sinfulness and temptation and vanity. It is stifled by women who buy into some unrealistic image and deny the beauty God bestowed on them.

I'M BRINGING SEXY BACK

Because God entrusted us with such a powerful gift, our responsibility is to steward it well. Your beauty is not to seduce men and make them stumble (unless it's your husband, then by all means). It is not a card to play carelessly. Nor should you deny it with self-loathing or endless comparisons.

Perhaps you refuse to acknowledge your own loveliness. Oh, how many beautiful women are stuck here! Maybe the magazines and movies have distorted your perspective. For that, I want to pull my hair out. I despise an industry that perpetuates an impossible image while playing on our insecurities. Plus, it's all a sham. My friend professionally consulted with Victoria's Secret, and it brought a mean thrill when he told us, "You should see their pictures before they're touched up. Any woman can be an underwear model with *that* technology!"

To look in the mirror and detest your image is to call God's handiwork a failure. Isaiah warned us,

What sorrow awaits those who argue with their Creator.
     Does a clay pot argue with its maker?
Does the clay dispute with the one who shapes it, saying,
     "Stop, you're doing it wrong!"
Does the pot exclaim,
     "How clumsy can you be?" (45:9, NLT, emphasis added).

While most believe sorrow over beauty comes from not having enough, God's Word says it's from getting crossways with His design.

Women experience that same brand of sorrow when they cling to guilt after they're forgiven, or when they decide they're useless though uniquely gifted for the kingdom, or they prefer staying broken when Jesus made them whole, or, of course, when they believe they are ugly when, in fact, they are the highlight of the earth.

Every woman is beautiful, each in her own way. The obsession with external perfection (whatever that is) only veils our beauty more. A woman who glows from the inside out, comfortable in her own skin, holds the gaze of every eye in the room, whether young or old, curvy or stick straight, built like a cheerleader or a linebacker.

If you are emotionally incapable of embracing your own beauty, it might help to acknowledge any way your beauty has been exploited. Perhaps you suffered abuse, and your physical beauty is a permanent reminder. Maybe you're terrified to look like a woman; you're conscious only of feeling ugly and have no idea that sexual exploitation made you terrified to be attractive to men. Perhaps you overcompensated for that injury and exploit or deface your own beauty now. If the idea of displaying your beauty makes you nauseous, you might ask yourself whether someone defiled your loveliness once.

If you spend your time acting invisible or marring your own beauty, understand that some wounds go far deeper than mind over matter. If your reaction to this section is violent or extreme, you might consider

Christian counseling to assist your heart in reconnecting with your body. Your beauty should not cause you unnecessary shame, grief, or horror; if it does, it is not your appearance that needs change but your heart.

Confession is defined as "saying the same thing as." For instance, when we say the same thing about our sin as God does, we've confessed it. It no longer hangs between us. The daughters of Christ need to confess their beauty. What did Christ say so we can agree?

> The king is enthralled by your beauty;
> honor him, for he is your lord. (Psalm 45:11)

TAKE MY HAND, TAKE MY WHOLE LIFE, TOO

Boaz was enthralled by Ruth's beauty too. "And now, my daughter, don't be afraid. I will do for you all you ask. All my fellow townsmen know that you are a woman of noble character." In every way, he affirmed her beauty; Boaz said yes to her loveliness. It trumped his desire to marry from the right stock. It overshadowed the scandal of falling in love with a woman in poverty. Beauty triumphed.

I'm sure Boaz received wise counsel from his mother, once a Canaanite prostitute, now a beauty of Israel. He was raised in a house of redemption, a lesson we should take note of as mothers. The next day, Boaz addressed the town elders on redeeming Elimelech's land and family. There was a kinsman-redeemer one degree closer, so Boaz put him to the question and made it clear he would redeem the land (and by the way, Ruth too, just to follow the rules and all) if this man were unwilling.

By chance, as it turned out, randomly, the other man passed.

Twenty-four hours after Ruth's request, Boaz made it official.

Ruth became a wife and mother, the titles she'd lost in Moab.

Naomi became a mother and grandmother, the titles she'd forfeited too. As Naomi held her grandson, Obed, the women declared, "May he become famous throughout Israel! He will renew your life and sustain you in your old age. For your daughter-in-law, who loves you and who is better to you than seven sons, has given him birth."

Obed fathered Jesse, who brought forth a son named David. Like his great-grandmother Ruth, and her mother-in-law Rahab, David was plucked from lowly, unlikely places and placed on the throne. Never in Israel was there such a king—a forerunner of the Messiah, man after God's own heart.

Through the union of this hero and his beauty, "David's fame spread throughout every land, and the LORD made all the nations fear him" (1 Chronicles 14:17). Zechariah said of the coming Christ through the same bloodline, "The LORD will be king over the whole earth. On that day there will be one LORD, and his name the only name" (Zechariah 14:9). Righteous fame was indeed delivered to God's anointed.

See one more thing, girls: This is how God described His ideal relationship with us:

> I spread the corner of my garment over you and covered your nakedness. I gave you my solemn oath and entered into a covenant with you, declares the Sovereign LORD, and you became mine.
>
> I bathed you with water and washed the blood from you and put ointments on you. I clothed you with an embroidered dress and put leather sandals on you. I dressed you in fine linen and covered you with costly garments. I adorned you with jewelry: I put bracelets on your arms and a necklace around your neck, and I put a ring on your nose, earrings on your ears and a beautiful crown on your head. So you were adorned with gold and silver; your clothes were of fine linen

and costly fabric and embroidered cloth. Your food was fine flour, honey and olive oil. You became very beautiful and rose to be a queen. And your fame spread among the nations on account of your beauty, *because the splendor I had given you made your beauty perfect*, declares the Sovereign LORD. (Ezekiel 16:8-14, emphasis added)

Glorious and full of splendor is a woman. You are perfectly beautiful, redeemed and displayed by Christ. And as lovely as the container is, the treasure within shines through, brilliant and blessed. Your physical beauty is a reflection of your soul and the likeness of your Savior. You wear His beauty well.

And if beauty means young, skinny, and flawless, then someone better tell my grandma, because at ninety-one, she is more beautiful than ever. The light of her Lord has increased in intensity and leaks out from a vessel that can no longer contain it. Oh, she's still painting the house, of course, but it's the lantern hanging firmly inside that radiates beauty and loveliness and glory, which age, sickness, and even death cannot extinguish.

And all God's women said, "Amen."

CHAPTER 8

Painful Subtraction

Suffering, Loss, and Other Things That Make or Break Us

Myth #4:

Godly women should be exempt from heartache.

2 Samuel 11–12

My Girlfriend Michelle confessed the funniest mom moment I've heard in a while. Her son Wesley was the classic firstborn: pleaser, compliant, well mannered, and basically easy to raise. (Don't you know God designed them like that so we'd continue to procreate? See all stories related to my youngest for why women stop.)

When Wesley turned five, something shifted. He started acting crazy! He threw fits and stomped his feet at Michelle. He was obstinate and hard to manage for no reason. The final straw happened at Home Depot when Michelle refused to buy him a playscape and Wesley threw an epic tantrum as she abandoned ship in horror. The ensuing discipline made matters worse, as Wesley declared himself hated and despised. This went on for two weeks.

Frustrated, Michelle recalled his behavior—tantrums, self-absorption, disobedience, dramatic overreactions—and she decided to handle this shocking conduct like any mother would:

She paid for Wesley to have an MRI.

I mean, after all, what five-year-old boy behaves like that? Throwing fits and whatnot! He *had* hit his head a couple of weeks back, and as a professional in the health-care industry, Michelle was convinced he had inner cranial trauma. For the bargain price of twelve hundred dollars, she discovered he was being a normal kindergartner, as boys his age are prone to do.

She told him afterward, "Guess what, mister? I *know* you don't have a brain injury. You're just being a stinker, and it's over." I call that the most expensive discipline ever. Cross Michelle and expect to get your five-year-old butt strapped down and stuffed into a radioactive tube for an hour with the threat of starting over if you move one inch.

Scared him straight too.

Just when life is coasting along, it often takes a surprising turn for the worse. A crisis rises out of thin air. An illness shows its face. A relationship is destroyed. The only thing worse than the heartache itself is that we didn't expect it, making it doubly traumatizing. We are unprepared to handle it, so a volatile reaction is all we can muster.

GOD'S GOLDEN BOY (MR. SHOULD NOT)

Suffering is universal, but it adopts added complications for a believer. With God in the equation, a list of "shoulds" materializes. Life for a Christian woman should go like this. It should not go like that. God should fix this situation, and He should not allow that one. This scenario should turn out like this. That group should not be permitted to triumph.

Let's meet the next woman in Jesus' lineage, Bathsheba, and learn about suffering on God's watch and how it affects our identities. Looking backward, we see two major benchmarks in the nation of God. For us, Jesus is our ultimate benchmark. He was the fulfillment of every hope professed before and after Him. All we believe about salvation was wrapped up in the person of Christ. He is the standard by which life and eternity are established. All that hung in the balance was finished in Jesus.

But until Christ, the end-all, be-all spiritual benchmark was King David. He was the dream come true. Any rabbinical literature will agree he represented the high point in Israeli history. He was a fearless fighter, taking down lions and giants. He molded a factious tribal group into a minor empire. Not only was he a brilliant warrior and city planner but he also had genuine star power. He was handsome and talented, a lover and a poet. When David took the throne, Israel transitioned into legitimacy. The security and international respect the Hebrews had longed for was realized under his leadership.

Scripture brags about King David book after book. He is introduced in 1 Samuel, and he's still getting line space in Revelation. Almost every New Testament writer referenced him; in fact, David's name is mentioned 970 times in Scripture. (Jesus beat him by only 306). David, David, David! Yeah, David! You're so cool! But one verse summing up David's legacy is worth noting:

> David had done what was pleasing in the LORD's sight and had obeyed the LORD's commands throughout his life, except in the affair concerning Uriah the Hittite. (1 Kings 15:5, NLT)

Not surprisingly, this disclaimer has something to do with our next female honoree. Out of the five women named in Jesus' family tree, Tamar, Rahab, and Ruth are honored as David's ancestors, and Mary is applauded for being his descendant. Only one woman was personally connected to David himself, and she suffered at his hands. I celebrate the authors and editors of Scripture; it must've been hard to include this account of their hero. This story reminds us that even the best saints are utterly human in their hurt, their hate, and their hope.

"I'M BORED. WHO CAN I SLEEP WITH?" — DAVID

It begins with David slacking off. He'd been established in Jerusalem for ten years, and "in the spring, at the time when kings go off to war, David sent Joab out with the king's men and the whole Israelite army. They destroyed the Ammonites and besieged Rabbah. But David remained in Jerusalem." The subheads in my Bible leading up to this point read: David Anointed King Over Judah, David Becomes King Over Israel, David Conquers Jerusalem, David Defeats the Philistines, David Brings the Ark to Jerusalem, God's Promise to David, David's Victories.

So much success, so much favor. As it has done for centuries, achievement corrupted the vessel, even one as good as David. A subtle shift took place in his heart. The kingdom that God trusted him to lead became *his* kingdom. The people he should've protected, he used for personal gain. The power he was to steward in humility became his weapon.

While his men were at war, David wandered the palace, bored and unoccupied, and he saw beautiful Bathsheba bathing close by. Not governed by discipline anymore, he sent someone to find out who she was. It was reported that she was the daughter of Eliam and the wife of Uriah the Hittite.

Here's why that information was included. Who were Eliam and Uriah to David? They were both honored members of "The Thirty," a select group of warriors comprising his royal guard. They uniquely protected David and were renowned for their valor. In other words, they were David's faithful bodyguards.

Let's go one step further. Eliam's father was David's top counselor, Ahithophel. Let that close connection sink in: Bathsheba's grandfather was David's closest advisor. These were not random men in the kingdom. They were heavily invested in David's success and protection. He owed not only his accomplishments but *his life* to their intervention.

So when he learned Bathsheba was the daughter, granddaughter, and wife of three essential men in his life, how did he respond? With integrity fitting a king? No, he had her brought to the palace where he slept with her and sent her home, violating her body while her husband was at war, where David was supposed to be. A one-night stand to satisfy his lust, Bathsheba was sent away as quickly as she'd been retrieved. There was no communication, no conversation. In fact, her only words recorded during this sickening affair were weeks later, when she sent word to David: "I am pregnant."

Heartbreak.

"THINGS I DESERVE FROM YOU, GOD — GET A PEN . . ."

If anyone "should've" been safe, it was Bathsheba. This "should" never have happened, considering her connections to David. She was on the king's side; surely she was protected. Yet none of her advantages sheltered her from a leader temporarily driven by ego and lust.

Girls, how many of us have suffered unexpectedly? All our connections and preventions failed us, and we endured a heartache we thought we were insulated from. The woman devoted to health is diagnosed with cancer; the dedicated mother loses a child; the sacrificial wife gets discarded for another woman; the unsuspecting girl is betrayed by her friend. There is hardly a crisis that women encounter that doesn't leave us reeling in shock.

The sheer injustice creates a tension sometimes more damaging than the disaster. That friction is often directed at God. "How could you allow this? You should have . . . You shouldn't have . . ." It's so unfair, so undeserved. Our hearts break under the strain of injustice.

We wouldn't readily admit it, but we carry a sense of entitlement as God's daughters. Because we belong to Him (serve Him, love Him, trust Him), we should receive only blessings and protection from suffering. It's only fair. It's kind of the deal we brokered at salvation: God, I'll give you this, this, and this, and You give me a happy life.

When the ground falls out, we sometimes shake an angry fist at Him for not protecting our happiness. We may quit praying or even quit God. I appreciate a young woman who attended our Bible study after a prolonged absence from Christ. She'd lost several high school friends in a tragic car accident, and the tragedy significantly damaged her. She said honestly, "I feel like I need to be here, but you should know that I hate God. He #&$%@! me up." When a crisis has no one to blame, God usually becomes the scapegoat.

Other women assume God is punishing them for some reason. We've done something to deserve this; it's a result of our deficiencies. We "should" have done this or "should not" have done that. So we cower in our spiritual corners, thinking how hard it is to get (or stay) on God's good side.

LIFE IS HARD. THE END.

Here is the truth: If your heart beats, you will suffer. It is part of the human condition. No amount of "shoulds" will change that. We own corrupted bodies in a corrupted world; we're plagued with sin, death, and decay; we are born to imperfect parents and have imperfect relationships; everyone gets sick and all of us will die. (Isn't this a fun paragraph?)

The prophet Habakkuk spiraled in frustration, stunned that God would not intervene in his suffering:

How long, O Lord, must I call for help,
    but you do not listen?
Or cry out to you, "Violence!"
    but you do not save?
Why do you make me look at injustice?
    Why do you tolerate wrong?
Destruction and violence are before me;
    there is strife, and conflict abounds. (1:2-3)

How could goodness be realized again? When would this night end? What could possibly explain God's silence?

God answered, "Look at the nations and watch—and be utterly amazed. For I am going to do something in your days that you would not believe, even if you were told" (verse 5). Maybe you can't imagine anything amazing from your heartache. It seems too far gone or the pain too intense. You've lost someone too soon or are betrayed beyond repair. The pain of humanity is that of heart, soul, passion, and emotions— easily injured and hard to heal.

God says, "Watch—and be utterly amazed."

I'm emerging from a season of suffering. The darkness fell through a severed relationship, entirely unexpected. The shock of turmoil and intensity it escalated was so painful, I wasn't sure I'd make it. Add a sense of injustice, powerlessness, and misrepresentation, and you have the recipe that left me with an ulcer, high blood pressure, and chronic abdominal pain. My body told me that my heart was not doing well.

For a while, all I did was survey the carnage, shocked at the damage. I'd study the damage, evaluate it, replay how it "should" have gone, teach the damage Scriptures I thought it needed to hear, mourn the damage. Then I thought ugly, mean thoughts good Christian women shouldn't think. I wrote scathing speeches in my head I'd never deliver. I cried endlessly, when I wasn't furious. I quit sleeping. I watered the carnage every day, making sure it was growing and vibrant. I gave it all my attention, pruning back parts that weren't developing, sprinkling the fertilizer of anguish and bitterness on it repeatedly.

Strangely, I wasn't feeling any better.

I told God, "Everything is ruined! How can I move forward now? How is this ever going to be okay?" And He told me so gently, so lovingly, "Watch Me and be amazed." God wooed me away from the damage I was diligently tending to, and He did things I couldn't believe, even if I'd been told.

It began with me, as these things often do. God asked the tough questions I hate: Whose approval do you really want? Who is your Provider? Who owns the cattle on a thousand hills? Who are you trying to please? Who can restore the worst breach? Whose plans will endure? Who are you placing your trust in? Who is in charge here? ("You," said the daughter sullenly.)

When I chose to watch, I saw Him.

I PREFER NIGHT IN ALASKA

God told Habakkuk,

> For the revelation awaits an appointed time;
> it speaks of the end
> and will not prove false.
> Though it linger, wait for it;
> it will certainly come and will not delay. (2:3)

God's victory over suffering, through suffering, in spite of suffering *will* be revealed. Pain is no match for His peace, sin has no authority over His rule. The lessons of the night are endurance, patience, dependence, and humility; they aren't products of the day.

In our blackest moments, God's glory shines brightest. It's when He can say, "I've been your Savior, but now you'll know me as Healer, Restorer, Sustainer." How else could we know Him like that? By day, many things clamor for our affection, but all a Christian wants in the night is her God. We experience single-minded devotion that sustains us in the night and changes how we live when the sun rises again.

After my relational turmoil, here is what I know:

- It is impossible to slip from God's hand.
- His opinion of me is all that matters.
- His plans for me cannot be thwarted.
- I'll never be the same.

Those lessons were expensive, but happiness in prosperity is cheap. God was there in my night, and the night changed me for the better.

The night falls on us all, girls. If it hasn't, just live longer. It isn't a question of why, though that is the answer we want. Suffering is no indicator of divine disfavor, dear one. The best of God's saints had their nights. Salvation doesn't insulate us from pain, but it does provide the Savior to deal with it.

That is the question to ask: What have you allowed God to do with your suffering? Are you still tending it, keeping it alive and thriving? Not sure? Check your body, check your inner dialogue. Those two clues point in the right direction. When I drift during misery, my body falls apart and the racket in my head makes me a crazy person.

This subject affects our feminine identity entirely. Women who nurture their suffering rather than their dependence on Christ become bitter, cynical, and broken. You know them. Whatever was once soft in them becomes hard and brittle; others shatter against them. Caustic, toxic, they deny everything that is lovely about a woman.

Victorious women are glory bearers for Christ. We represent the majesty of the King when we bravely let Him heal us. "These women don't give a testimony of what God can do," wrote Jacqueline Jakes. "These women *are* a testimony of what He can do. Trophy Women are eyewitnesses to the deliverance of God. They are women whom life has cast down but who have risen up with fists filled with glory from real encounters with God."[1]

Lord, how I want to be that. Women who fight the good fight and finish strong, refusing to live defeated lives—these girls do God proud. You have a triumphant spirit, sister. Look at the Christ you were patterned after. The sun has risen on many daughters of God, revealing women refined through their night. They've had a hands-on experience with the Almighty, and their faces glow with His glory. They emerge with new battle scars, but those are marks of honor, evidence of victory.

Who are you going to be?

KING DAVID'S HANDIWORK: A TRAGEDY IN THREE ACTS

Sometimes suffering gets worse before it gets better. After a forced sexual encounter with the king while her husband was at war, Bathsheba was pregnant and dishonored. When David heard, he reacted like so many when faced with their sin. Rather than confess his mistake and move forward in integrity, he engineered a cover-up that went dreadfully awry.

David sent for Bathsheba's husband, Uriah, pretending to want an update on the battle. After that fake conversation, he told Uriah to go home for the night, hoping he'd sleep with Bathsheba and eliminate the inevitable raised eyebrows when she turned up pregnant with a husband at war. But, as a man of honor, Uriah slept outside the palace by the servants; his conscience would not allow him sexual pleasure while "the ark and Israel and Judah are staying in tents, and my master Joab and my lord's men are camped in the open fields. How could I go to my house to eat and drink and lie with my wife?"

Touché.

Plan B: David invited Uriah to stay in the palace that night, got him drunk, and hoped he'd feel spicy and go home. He did not. He slept by the servants again, a repeat of the night before but with a nasty hangover.

Backed into a corner, drunk with power, David had Uriah placed on the front lines of battle and the soldiers withdrew and left him alone to die. Better a murder than a scandal. No sooner was Uriah buried than David made Bathsheba another one of his many wives. The raped widow was whisked to the palace, without one person to defend her.

So God stepped into the story.

SILENCE OF THE LAMB

"The LORD sent Nathan to David." Nathan, dear and brave prophet, brought David a tale of a poor man who had only one lamb. He loved his little lamb, and it "even slept in his arms." A rich man lived nearby who owned tons of sheep and cattle. When a traveler visited the rich man, rather than prepare a meal with one of his many sheep, he took the poor man's one lamb, leaving him empty-handed. The end.

David was livid. "As surely as the LORD lives, the man who did this deserves to die! He must pay for that lamb four times over, because he did such a thing and had no pity." Sin blinds us so. When Nathan explained that David was the rich man, Uriah the poor man, and Bathsheba the stolen lamb, David's heart broke with guilt. Nathan told him that his mistake was forgiven but that the son Bathsheba bore would die. She lost her honor, her husband, and her only son because of one man's wayward power.

This story is more than we want to know about David, but let it also be a story of God's intervention in the lives of His daughters. God's power was greater than David's, and He defended the cause of the oppressed. The loved and stolen lamb compelled the God of the universe to intervene.

And what intervention! Bathsheba's plight inspired words from a prophet. Discipline was administered to the king whose power had begun to stink. Though forgiven for the miscarriage of justice, this offense began a downward spiral for David and his family; he did not escape the consequences of sin, murder, and deceit. Finally, God blessed Bathsheba with a second son, whose wisdom and wealth have never been matched.

JUSTICE OF ANOTHER LAMB

The prophets said of Jesus,

> In love a throne will be established;
> in faithfulness a man will sit on it —
> one from the house of David —
> one who in judging seeks justice
> and speeds the cause of righteousness. (Isaiah 16:5)

In Christ, all the wrongs will ultimately be made right. Every injustice will be exposed and redeemed. The oppressed will be defended, as they always have been on His watch.

In Jesus' lineage it reads, "David was the father of Solomon, whose mother had been Uriah's wife." Now, that's interesting. At Solomon's birth, Bathsheba was David's wife, yet God reminds us that as revered as David was, he's not the star in this lineage. David—the man after God's heart, the best of Israel's kings—he's the guy who forcibly seduced another guy's wife. The only star in this lineage is Jesus. Jesus never abused power or abused women; He welcomed them as His disciples. Jesus didn't use war and deception to show strength; He demonstrated only peace in the face of delusion. Jesus refused to play by the rules of power politics, and he will never fail us as our King.

God included unlikely contributors in Jesus' family tree—the likes of Tamar, Rahab, Ruth, and Bathsheba. At the same time, He selected the gem of the group and gently reminded us through careful wording that no one is worthy without a Savior, not even King David.

Let us again bow reverently to grace, because the God who cried for Bathsheba and kept her in the salvation story also allowed David to remain in it too. Suffering is terribly human; sometimes it is the death and decay we all endure, sometimes it's at the hands of another, and sometimes we cause it for someone else.

God will bring judgment when He has to, but He'd rather work redemption. Before He resorts to vengeance, He'll try mercy. The Lord stays His hand—longer than we want for those who injure us, and longer than we could hope for our own shortcomings—to bring us to repentance.

Dear daughter, take heart. All suffering can be turned into salvation in the hands of God. He can heal your damage if you'll let Him. He'll walk with you in your night, working miracles you couldn't imagine during the day. Astonishingly, He can turn your heartache into your ministry, your passion. Our greatest gifts are birthed out of our greatest injuries.

He releases our healed spirits, ministering on His behalf and delivering compassion to those walking the paths we've traveled. How could we carry on Jesus' mission if His people only knew happiness and prosperity? How could we minister? How could we possibly understand? How could we wrap our arms around someone and say, "I've been there. God brought me through"?

Invite Him into your night, and He'll walk you back into the day. That humility, that dependence, is a lesson of darkness, and He won't short-circuit your maturity by coming uninvited. I don't know what you've suffered, but don't underestimate what God can do with it. You may be in a dark night of the soul, but "for you who revere my name, the sun of righteousness will rise with healing in its wings" (Malachi 4:2).

Watch for that sunrise, sister.

CHAPTER 9

The Theory of Multiplication

Why Holler When You Can Purr?

Truth #4:

Women have the gift of influence.

1 Kings 1–2

I'm going to make a confession: I'm a closet granola-type. I'm not going to lie; I read labels. Don't get me wrong: I'll pick up drive-through quicker than you can say "partially hydrogenated oil," but *All Natural* shows up in my kitchen more than I'd like to admit. (My reluctance to divulge this is due to the annoying/condescending air of most granola foodies, such as, "Oh, I never give that to Bella Elizabeth and Cole Michael. I grow and can all their vegetables.") Well, la dee da.

However, my kids are very aware of my organic tendencies. They even read labels. My five-year-old, Caleb, reported good news after his brother read some ingredients: "Guess what, Mom! These cookies won't give us cancer!" (Insert husband rolling eyes and shaking head here.)

Listen, I'm not ashamed to brainwash my children.

Anytime I call home while traveling, they narc: "We've had no vegetables since you left." They tattle about the fast-food restaurants Daddy took them to for every meal. Obviously, these opposite parenting techniques create confusion. Caleb asked, "Why doesn't Daddy want us to be healthy? I don't think he wants me to get stronger than him."

Score one for mom's influence.

However, over dinner recently, my girlfriends and I got on the topic of screwing up our kids. As we are their primary influence, it's basically inevitable. We went around the table predicting what our kids would one day say to their therapists:

"My mom was wound tighter than a spool of yarn."
"My mom loved cleaning more than she loved her children."
"My mom screamed like a monkey on meth."
"My mom locked us in the backyard."
"My mom traveled and terrified us with cancer warnings."

Lord help us. A woman's influence is so strong. When it's not used for good, it's therapy material. Just like our beauty, our influence is powerful, never neutral. It is the invisible gift we overlook. Surrounded by struggle and conflict, women hold the key to reconciliation.

PALACE DRAMA

We have such an example in Bathsheba. Although the first chapter of her story records only three words, we meet her personally later. Biblically, we have two more encounters with her, both demonstrating her influence. One is worthy of eternal repetition, and the other is a warning for her feminine descendants. Let it be said: Influence is either stewarded for righteousness or mishandled for destruction.

Fast-forward a generation. Bathsheba's son Solomon is a young man, and David is on his deathbed. And lest you assume David wasn't disciplined for his treatment of "Uriah's wife," death and conflict never left his household, just as Nathan prophesied. His family was plagued with incest, murder, conspiracy, and war. A rot set in through David's sin that took the lives of David's two oldest sons, while Bathsheba's son Solomon enjoyed God's favor.

When Solomon was little, David delivered this prophetic promise:

My son, I had it in my heart to build a house for the Name of the Lord my God. But this word of the Lord came to me: "You have shed much blood and have fought many wars. You are not to build a house for my Name, because you have shed much blood on the earth in my sight. But you will have a son who will be a man of peace and rest, and I will give him rest from all his enemies on every side. His name will be Solomon, and I will grant Israel peace and quiet during his reign. He is the one who will build a house for my Name. He will be my son, and I will be his father. And I will establish the throne of his kingdom over Israel forever." (1 Chronicles 22:7-10)

God gave Bathsheba a gem of a son.

Don't forget what that meant for her: She would be Israel's Queen Mother, an influential position in the royal court, when the nation's glory was at its highest point. This was a true honor, as David had at least eight wives, nineteen sons, and more unnamed according to the Chronicles. Only one wife would become Queen Mother, and God promised that title to Bathsheba. The stolen lamb would become a queen.

So imagine the panic when David's son Adonijah took advantage of David's failing health and declared himself king. Why not? David was about to die, and he was the oldest son still alive. So he gathered conspirators, threw himself a party, left David's supporters and Solomon off the guest list, and claimed the throne.

This was a crisis, girls. Twenty years earlier, David would've routed this conspiracy and reclaimed justice for Solomon. But now he was at death's door. The cries from the street were, "Long live King Adonijah!" The priests, military commanders, royal family, and royal officers were all in on it. There was no one left to secure Solomon's legacy. History teetered on the balance, and the throne of Israel seemed lost from God's favored successor.

PLANET DRAMA

We, too, are surrounded by conflict on every side. Perhaps a monarchy doesn't hang in the balance, but maybe a marriage does. Injustice prevails; the oppressed have few advocates. God's purposes are jeopardized everywhere. His dreams for healthy families, faithful marriages, and godly children are in trouble; eighteen thousand children die of hunger *daily* in a world of plenty[1]; millions of people perish for lack of inexpensive medicines; violence is the parent of the streets; poverty-induced genocide claims innocents; the church has gone dormant. Paul wrote, "The whole creation has been groaning as in the pains of childbirth right up to the present time" (Romans 8:22). What does creation look forward to? "The creation waits in eager expectation for the sons of God to be revealed" (verse 19).

"I sense a slow and steady collapse," wrote Lisa Bevere. "The surrounding forces exerting themselves are greater than our inward constitution can endure. Families are fragmented, nations are divided, government and financial institutions are crumbling. Creation is not well. Its guardians and keepers have left their posts. If our reckless choices have brought destruction, doesn't it stand to reason we can be part of the restoration?"[2]

As daughters of the King, we hold sway over the struggles in the kingdom. Whether the battle is on a micro or macro level, God positions women to bring healing. You are not benign, and the sidelines are for those who lack vision. The world is not a mess because of God's abdication. I call as my witnesses millions of women wringing their hands, wishing they could do something.

All the while, they are the answer everyone is looking for.

THE SECRET WEAPON

Nathan heard of Adonijah's arrogant move. Don't you know he felt the same panic? This was a catastrophe, and the usual players were out of commission. Who was going to fix this? Who would speak rationally? Who could be the hero? Technically, only David could reverse this calamity. As a bona fide prophet, Nathan possessed supernatural discernment. Who should he enlist? David historically used force, but Nathan's weapon was always wisdom.

Enter Bathsheba.

Nathan told her, "Let me advise you how you can save your own life and the life of your son Solomon. Go in to King David and say to him, 'My lord the king, did you not swear to me your servant: "Surely Solomon your son shall be king after me, and he will sit on my throne"? Why then has Adonijah become king?' While you are still there talking to the king, I will come in and confirm what you have said."

The throne was usurped; lives were at stake; David's legacy was in jeopardy. So God's prophet—privy to the wisdom of heaven—advised a woman to use her influence over a man. That was the great divine answer. Between God, His Spirit, wisdom, and experience, Nathan determined that the best tool was feminine persuasion; his confirmation would only be the exclamation point.

"To try and give honor to women in the sweep of history is impossible here," wrote the Eldredges in *Captivating*. "It would be easier to think of any of the great or small turning points in God's rescue of mankind and try to find one where women were *not* irreplaceable. . . . Your lingering disbelief that anything important hangs on your life is only evidence of the long assault on your heart by the one who knows who you could be and fears you."[3]

A woman affects a man's soul, changing his mind, his direction, his life. Through your gentle advice and godly suggestions, God can rend a man's heart. Why? Isn't it so obvious by now?

A man stands to gain much from a godly woman. Experience tells him her intuition is usually spot-on. She reads the nuances of a situation with precision, discerning subtleties hidden from the naked eye. She knows what people are thinking and predicts how they will respond. She speaks not just toward what is smart but what is right. You are a trustworthy counselor, sister. Men realize your intelligence and intuition, your courage and calling. As my Girlfriend Laura told me yesterday, "I genuinely think I know what is best for, well, everyone." Guess what? Nine times out of ten, she does.

And don't forget that little thing you are, called "beautiful." Your man heeds your suggestions because he wants you. He is mesmerized by you. Your beauty is incentive in itself. Don't mistake that as a bad thing. God figured out this formula long ago. ("Hmmm, how can I get my men to listen to my women . . . ?") Your man wants *you* to want *him*, and acting foolishly against your sound advice is not a good start. He desires your favor and respect. When you believe in him, all is right in his world.

HOW WE ARE LIKE GAVIN THE ULTIMATE

It reminds me of my sons. Gavin, nine, represents every goodness in the universe to Caleb, five. He is the ultimate human being. Caleb's favorite number? Nine, Gavin's age. Caleb's favorite name? Gavin, what he plans to change his name to when he turns eighteen. When my oldest was away at camp, Caleb buried his head in my shoulder and cried, "Nothing is good without Gavin." When Gavin returned, Caleb told him, "I've had a headache all week from missing you."

There is nothing Caleb won't do for him. He helps clean his room; he buys Gavin's art projects; he'll be the "pet" when they play. Gavin's opinion of him is everything.

In fact, the night before Caleb started kindergarten, Gavin told me, "Mom, I'm so worried. I just know Caleb will be the bully at school. I want to pray about it." (These are concerns you hear from firstborns.) Caleb overheard that, tucking it away as truth. So when he jumped off the bus the first day of school, the first thing he said was, "Mom! Guess what! I wasn't even the bully today!" He was certain Gavin's prediction was a fact, stunned it turned out false. Still, he remains a devoted fan, willing to do anything for Gavin's approval.

This is like our power, girls. Its intensity is stronger than our men let on. If we misuse it, we will answer for it someday. Bathsheba gives a shining example of how to steward our influence, particularly with men.

R-E-S-P-E-C-T, FIND OUT WHAT IT MEANS TO . . . HIM

She went to David and "bowed low and knelt before the king." Let's stop there. Don't freak out; you don't have to bow. But a good principle holds, like it or not. Everyone knows a man's love language is respect. It is infinitely more effective than its inferior cousins: nagging, controlling, and demanding. This emotional posture tells a man, "I'm not here to criticize you. I believe in you. I have no plans to dominate you."

Notice Bathsheba began like this. Respect comes first. It eliminates the threat of emasculation right away. Start a conversation with your finger in a man's face and see how far you get. A man's going in a questionable direction (or no direction) doesn't give us the right to shame him because "we know better." Hold respect in one hand and you can bring wisdom in the other.

The wise in heart are called discerning,
and pleasant words promote instruction. (Proverbs 16:21)

Men deserve to be treated with dignity as much as women do. What love does for a woman, respect does for a man. It disarms him and prepares him to hear truth without the static of defensiveness. When God prompts you to influence a man, check your body language, heed your tone. One glance at you should communicate respect, not contempt.

PROMISE KEEPERS (LOSERS WEEPERS)

"My lord, you yourself swore to me your servant by the LORD your God: 'Solomon your son shall be king after me, and he will sit on my throne.'" Bathsheba reminded David of his promise before exposing Adonijah's conspiracy.

Being considered a man of his word is huge to a guy. No man wants to be known as a slacker, a poser, or a joke. Honor is a commodity to a real man. Gently recalling a man's commitment is a discerning move. He didn't give his word lightly, and he won't quickly abandon it. Plus, time and conflict create a fuzzy memory. A clear calling can get blurred and even forgotten.

Sometimes women need to remind men of their covenants as husbands, fathers, and sons of God. Good: "You have always made me feel safe as your wife." Bad: "Your last good day was our wedding day, and since then, you've gotten dumber than a sack of diapers." Good: "Your promise to raise our kids together gave me courage to become a mother." Bad: "If you don't get out of that Barcalounger and help with bedtime, I'm changing my name to Lorena Bobbitt."

Men want to be men of their word, so sometimes we need to remind them what it was.

LEADING THE WITNESS: IT'S NOT JUST FOR LAWYERS

"But now Adonijah has become king, and you, my lord the king, do not know about it. He has sacrificed great numbers of cattle, fattened calves, and sheep, and has invited all the king's sons, Abiathar the priest and Joab the commander of the army, but he has not invited Solomon your servant." Notice Bathsheba presented the facts and held the commentary.

Brilliant.

A woman's best asset is how she sees the facts plainly. We think our job is to "help" men draw conclusions, but they aren't idiots. He can read the writing on the wall; a woman just directs his eyes there. Bathsheba simply told David who was invited and who wasn't, and the inference was obvious: Adonijah was staging a coup.

Girls, I love women so, but let me say this: All our yammering and explanations drive men crazy. What if Bathsheba said slowly, "Now, David, Adonijah invited these guys but didn't invite those guys. What do you see? My little eye spies a scheme. It seems he left off those who might expose him, and he invited the yes men. In other words, this was a deceptive, malicious plan. Do you understand? I know it's hard to believe, but this is a c-o-n-s-p-i-r-a-c-y. I'm not being condescending;

I'm just talking down to you."

Influence knows when to shut up. Tell a man the facts and then hush. Let him reach the obvious conclusion without insulting his intelligence. Less is more, girls. Less is also more effective. Once a man starts feeling lectured, it's over. Wise women stop short of telling men what to do. Give him the chance to be moved by your observations without being shoved by your condescension.

"YOU'RE THE MAN"

"My lord the king, the eyes of all Israel are on you, to learn from you who will sit on the throne of my lord the king after him." Bathsheba nodded to David's authority, reminding him of those under his leadership. At this point, Bathsheba is the savviest communicator I've ever seen.

If respect is a man's love language, then authority is his bread and butter. This dynamic has bothered women to no end. Women misunderstand the masculine desire for authority just as men misinterpret the feminine quest for beauty. Rather than embracing how men are wired, we've focused on how some have misused their position.

The truth is, God gave men authority knowing most would bend over backward to steward it well. When women call it forth rather than criticize or dominate, authority blesses those under it. Only when they are emasculated do good men resort to intimidation or resignation. By recognizing a man's authority, a woman affects how he treats her. He'll either protect his biggest fan or dominate his closest adversary.

(This, of course, doesn't hold true for all men. Like I mentioned in chapter 2, some men were deeply damaged before we got to them. Intimidation or resignation was etched into their patterns of life, regardless of how much love and respect they later receive. An abusive man won't ever steward his authority in a good way no matter how well you treat him.)

If you're getting mad, just stop it. Would you criticize a man for telling his wife she was beautiful, knowing she needed to hear it? Aren't all compliments offered to build up the hearer? If we expect men to communicate love for us in certain ways, then we should do the same.

Men are patterned after Jesus, who had all the authority in the world but used it to serve. The only time Jesus got testy about His authority was when it was challenged by fools. Outside of that, Jesus used His position to heal, forgive, and love everyone who came to Him. That same design compels men to offer what every woman wants: protection, provision, and security.

We activate a vicious cycle when we dominate men. They feel defensive, so they act more aggressively, and then we become furious and more resistant. Don't think I'm advocating some backward, male-dominated society where women should just put out and shut up. Domination is not godly for either gender; the same cycle happens when men control women. This is simply practical advice going with our grain rather than against it.

Think of it in feminine terms. We want our men to love us well. We want to feel appreciated and adored. Men read this in their books and hear it from their teachers, too. So much of that is hard for them; they aren't expressive by nature. If they decided we were too needy, this whole dynamic too hard, and they ignored our longings on principle, would that be effective? Would we eventually decide they were right? No! We'd wither on the vine or find another man who acknowledged our value.

Don't forget: You may recognize his authority, but you still have influence. This whole thing works together. As Scripture says, mutual submission is central to marriage. We respect them; they love us. We keep their masculinity intact; they heed our every word. Our influence is used with wisdom; their authority is exercised with integrity. We affect how our men treat us. Many a suffering wife waits for her husband to change, while she holds the key to restoration.

"YOU'RE MY MAN"

One last lesson from Bathsheba: "Otherwise, as soon as my lord the king is laid to rest with his fathers, I and my son Solomon will be treated as criminals." Predicting the inevitable mistreatment by Adonijah, for whom Solomon was a threat, Bathsheba invoked the protector in David as the final exclamation point. If all else failed, this wouldn't.

Imagine me applauding Bathsheba's incredible use of her influence. This is genius. As a man wants respect and authority, he also totally wants to be the hero. Men were created to protect their people. You cross my husband, he is patient, but if you cross his wife, it's on. My dad was the same way. (Here I'd like to apologize to every coach, school counselor, teacher, and boss that ever foolishly caused me heartache. My dad's wrath was unforgettable.)

"True femininity arouses true masculinity," wrote the Eldredges. "Think about it—all those heroes in all those tales play the hero because there is a woman in his life, a true Beauty who is his inspiration. It's that simple and that profound. We awaken it, arouse it in a way that nothing else on earth even comes close to."[4]

With all our feminism and girl power, we've forgotten to give men a reason to fight for us. We handle our own battles, thank you. So many men shrink away or assert their position because they don't feel needed. There is no one to protect, no one needs the hero in them. We make them feel there is nothing we can't do without them. They are a thorn in the sides of our competence. *Vulnerability* is a dirty word for our generation. Might as well call us helpless.

My girlfriend was struggling with her husband at home. She

was buckling under the crushing pressure of raising kids alone. Her husband was entirely disengaged. For months she begged and nagged. She yelled and screamed. She made chore charts and lists. She resorted to hostility and bawling. Nothing worked.

Then she sat down calmly with her husband, looked him gently in the eyes, and said, "I need you so badly. Only one person in the world can help me, and it's you. I'm sorry for how I've made you feel and how I've acted, but I feel so alone. I can't do it. I need you."

Bam! He engaged.

There is a hero in every man. The brilliant woman inspires him to show up. Reject the idea that vulnerability is weakness. It simply creates space for intimacy and stirs a man to offer his strength. When a woman uses her influence for healing and a man uses his might for justice, everyone wins.

After Bathsheba spoke with David, Nathan validated her report. From the mouths of two witnesses, truth and action were established. Reminded of his promise, informed of the facts, recognized for his authority, and asked for protection, David stayed death and became the warrior one last time. The influence of his bride inspired him to move immediately. Solomon was anointed with oil, paraded through the city, and placed on the throne. He was endorsed by King David, ensuring his succession.

"Then King David said, 'Call in Bathsheba.' So she came into the king's presence and stood before him. The king then took an oath: 'As surely as the LORD lives, who has delivered me out of every trouble, I will surely carry out today what I swore to you by the LORD, the God of Israel: Solomon your son shall be king after me, and he will sit on my throne in my place.'"

Powerful indeed.

YOU ARE A TARGET — DON'T BE DUMB (I MEANT THAT NICELY)

However, just as men have misused their strength, we women have distorted our influence. Trouble always plagues the powerful gifts. Even Bathsheba, after using her influence so wisely, fell into the trap of manipulation days later. May her example instruct and warn us today.

Adonijah, slighted altogether, devised a backdoor into the monarchy. According to ancient customs, a claim to power was solidified by taking the predecessor's wife. Succeed him in bed, succeed him on the throne. David took a young wife late in life, Abishag, whose primary role was caring for his health. They were never sexual, but she was a wife, nonetheless. Adonijah suspected the woman who secured Solomon's throne might also be his best chance. Influence the father, influence the son.

"Now Adonijah, the son of Haggith, went to Bathsheba, Solomon's mother. Bathsheba asked him, 'Do you come peacefully?'

"He answered, 'Yes, peacefully.' Then he added, 'I have something to say to you.'

"'You may say it,' she replied."

Let's stop here. Girls, your influence attracts both friend and foe. As much as God wants to use it for righteousness, the Enemy would use it for destruction. Its power is only as good as its intentions. Women must guard against all who would abuse its potency.

Satan tempted Eve first, but I disagree with fools who blame women's weakness and susceptibility. I don't believe Eve's weakness drew him; it was her strength. If he could mislead the neck, she'd turn the head. This is not a design flaw in women. I cite hundreds of biblical instances when men were manipulated for evil too. All humanity is vulnerable to deception, and the Creation story is no indicator of a gender defect. Rather, it demonstrates Satan's awareness of the feminine power of influence.

Bathsheba should've recognized Adonijah as an enemy. She

was dangerously naïve here. He had stolen the throne from her son through a conspiracy. She questioned his intentions but failed to discern the truth. She should've busted him so fast, he'd forever regret manipulating her influence for selfish gain.

Daughters, guard your influence like the treasure it is. Be aware of the Enemy, who would use it for harm. Our influence should be used only for healing, love, restoration, justice, righteousness, and goodness. The end. If we are tempted to use it for anything less, our radar should go up immediately.

HOW TO SPOT A PLAYER (AS ILLUSTRATED BY ADONIJAH)

Here are the warning signs to watch for:

"'As you know,' Adonijah said, 'the kingdom was mine. All Israel looked to me as their king. But things changed, and the kingdom has gone to my brother; for it has come to him from the LORD. Now I have one request to make of you. Do not refuse me.'

"'You may make it,' she said."

What did he play on, girls? Her compassion and the power of her position, conveniently twisting the facts in the process. "God gave my kingdom away, Bathsheba. Only you can help me regain this one little thing." We've got to recognize when we're being played. Just as enemies know our strengths, they realize our soft spots, too. Push the right button in a woman, and your chances increase dramatically. When anyone asks you to use your influence over another, don't disengage your mind from your heart. A person of dubious motives requires a second, third, and fourth assessment. Never enter an agreement with anyone who might use your influence as a weapon.

Be aware of your blind spots. When someone is playing to your pet passion, your favorite issue, or any characteristic that might overshadow your shrewdness, beware. Recognize flattery when it comes with a selfish agenda. Women feel their feelings very strongly, and don't think our enemies don't know it.

HOW TO BE A PLAYER (AS ILLUSTRATED BY BATHSHEBA)

"So he continued, 'Please ask King Solomon—he will not refuse you—to give me Abishag the Shunammite as my wife.'

"'Very well,' Bathsheba replied, 'I will speak to the king for you.'

"When Bathsheba went to King Solomon to speak to him for Adonijah, the king stood up to meet her, bowed down to her and sat down on his throne. He had a throne brought for the king's mother, and she sat down at his right hand.

"'I have one small request to make of you,' she said. 'Do not refuse me.'

"The king replied, 'Make it, my mother; I will not refuse you.'

"So she said, 'Let Abishag the Shunammite be given in marriage to your brother Adonijah.'"

Here we go. This thing started with faulty logic, which ensured it would not end well. Influence for evil or selfish gain is called manipulation. It uses different tactics and has different results. Notice how Bathsheba handled Solomon. It was just a "small request," and "Don't refuse me." She laid the foundation to get her way. We don't see the respect or wisdom she used with David. Her wording turned manipulative, angling for Solomon's compliance based on her position, not wisdom, not justice, not God's will.

"Manipulation strikes at the heart of a man through intimidation or seduction, thus coercing subjects to respond according to your desire and against their will," wrote Michelle McKinney Hammond.[5] Ungodly means never accomplish godly purposes. It's that simple. If our influence involves deception, seduction, or domination, we have derailed. These tactics are used to control someone rather than lead him to godliness, and there is a big difference.

Does the line seem blurry? Look at the results. The manipulated always become bitter toward the manipulators, because the manipulated come out losers. They are plagued with a sense of helplessness or dependency, humiliation and inadequacy. They either rage or retreat. Manipulation is ugly.

Look at the difference in Bathsheba's encounter with Solomon:

"King Solomon answered his mother, 'Why do you request Abishag the Shunammite for Adonijah? You might as well request the kingdom for him — after all, he is my older brother — yes, for him and for Abiathar the priest and Joab son of Zeruiah (the other conspirators)!'"

Where David acted immediately on Bathsheba's advice, Solomon became furious and lost respect for her. He responded with anger and sarcasm, shocked at his mother's foolishness. Rather than goodness, Bathsheba's manipulation produced a sharp rebuke. This is the last account we have of her.

Don't be deceived, girls: Manipulation doesn't really work. It may produce short-term results, but the cost is high and the consequences inevitable. Had Solomon followed her advice, Adonijah would have had a legitimate claim to the throne. At minimum, a violent power struggle would have robbed years of their lives, if not their very lives.

USING IT WITHOUT ABUSING IT

Be certain your influence supports God's holy standards before you use it or allow anyone else to borrow it. In the end, God's purposes will stand. So when we persuade others toward holiness, toward goodness, we divinely align ourselves. We can expect positive reactions and active responses. God supports what He approves. We have a heavenly ally in Christ when we affect hearts for righteousness.

I've seen women influence the direction of a man, a child, a family, a whole church, an entire city, even on national and international levels. One woman says, "There is a better way." One wife says, "We can no longer stay silent." One mother says, "It's time to reclaim our children." One daughter says, "I have a vision for peace." One sister says, "This is not the way of Christ." May we never forfeit that influence, mistakenly believing it's not enough.

You are a mighty tool in the hands of God, daughter. Your influence is nearly irresistible. Let's be the generation who won't surrender their position or use it for harm. May we rise up together, amazing women of Christ, and inspire change, justice, holiness, and strength in every life we touch.

If you are in the equation, there is hope yet.

Robert Kennedy said,

> Let no one be discouraged by the belief there is nothing one man or one woman can do against the enormous array of the world's ills—against misery and ignorance, injustice and violence. . . . Few will have the greatness to bend history itself; but each of us can work to change a small portion of events, and in the total of all those acts will be written the history of this generation. . . .
>
> It is from the numberless diverse acts of courage and belief that human history is shaped. Each time a man (or woman) stands up for an ideal, or acts to improve the lot of others, or strikes out against injustice, he (or she) sends a tiny ripple of hope, and crossing each other from a million different centers of energy and daring, those ripples build a current which can sweep down the mightiest walls of oppression and resistance.[6]

May the legacy of our generation declare the righteous power of our influence.

CHAPTER 10

Rounding Down

Why Thirty Is the New Fifty

Myth #5:

Spiritual maturity can only come with age.

LUKE I

Let me share the worst moment of my career to date. I was asked to keynote the Central Texas Women's Conference. Super. Sounded lovely. The invite came from a reputable source, so I agreed. Because it was close, I drove to a predetermined location, where my hostess picked me up. From there we took her car.

We drove farther and farther off the beaten path until we were straight-up in the boondocks. I started looking for Reverend Jonathan Whirley from *Dragnet*. We reached the "conference," which was a little house in the woods. Yes, it was. Picture this: I'm dressed to the nines, having spent days on my message, and I walk into a room with eight women in it—the youngest in her late fifties, the oldest about to die any second.

I was twenty-nine.

Dear girls, I couldn't make this up: Three of the women were in wheelchairs, computer paper was taped together and draped across the fireplace declaring this the "CENTRAL TEXAS WOMEN'S CONFERENCE" (a loose term, written in marker), and no one spoke to me. Oh, it gets worse.

During "worship," we sang one of my favorite preschool songs: "Hallelu, hallelu, hallelu, hallelujah! Praise ye the Lord!" Four of us stood during the *hallelus*, and the other four stood during the *Praise ye the Lords*. Then we switched, never forgetting the refrain ("Praise ye the Lord! Hallelujah!"). The wheelchair girls just raised their arms, naturally, as standing was a bit dicey. We sang this song six times, so help me, Jesus.

While I was teaching, one of the wheelchair grandmas fell asleep so violently, her snoring reverberated like a pug dog with asthma. People fall asleep all the time during sermons, but they aren't usually one of eight listeners four feet from the speaker. Between the snoring, the cynical body language, and my overstated outfit, I think I lost consciousness a couple of times. It was like an out-of-body experience. In the middle of my message, I was already planning the order of people to call from my car.

When I finished teaching, did I receive a thank-you? A word of appreciation? Oh, no. I got an earful in front of everyone on how I misinterpreted Scripture on not being slaves to the Law anymore ("I'll remind you, *young thing*, that Jesus said, 'Not the smallest letter, not the least stroke of a pen, will by any means disappear from the Law until everything is accomplished.'").

Great merciful heavens.

This conference taught me to ask specifics about an event before coming. I have only one Central Texas Women's Conference in me per decade, I think. (This was closely rivaled by the convention where the speaker before me delivered an hour-long rant against white people as I sat praying for the Rapture.)

GREEN IS ALWAYS GOLD, SOMETIMES

Ah, young versus old. It's a rub with many complexities. I'm thirty-three, so I've been young my whole life. I began feeling that tension in my twenties, and from age twenty-five on, I told people I was "about thirty." Turning thirty was such a relief; I figured people might finally take me seriously.

Youth has a schizophrenic following. On one hand, there is nothing women won't rub on, ingest, peel, or lift to reclaim it. The American anti-aging industry will reach nearly seventy-two billion dollars by 2009.[1] Consider that nine billion dollars would solve the planet's water crisis, and you can gauge our Western priorities. Green is gold, in terms of our health, skin, and pre-pregnancy bodies, God bless their memory.

But beyond skin deep, young people are marginalized for being too idealistic, too naïve, too inexperienced, and too transient. Age often disqualifies a girl—too young to be of real value or wisdom. She has nothing to offer; better to sit quiet and be a good girl. Young women receive the message loud and clear.

High school is practically infancy; focus on college. In college, build your resumé and make contacts for your upcoming career. Sandwich in graduate school to further prepare you for "later." Professionally, expect an entry-level position to guarantee future promotions. In fact, this company is just a front door for that next one. In the meantime, you're not ready for a relationship. You're not ready for leadership. You're not ready for a vision. The whole process enforces this message: Not yet . . . someday.

God constantly blows the doors off our stereotypes, whether history, pedigree, geography, nationality, or age. No one is more unconventional than God. Funny how His name is used to create boundaries when, in fact, He is the Ultimate Rebel. Frankly, I'm shocked when He uses anyone slightly normal, whatever that is.

HAS GOD DONE LOST HIS MIND?

We've come to the last woman named in Jesus' lineage. Each has gotten progressively closer to the Savior. Tamar lived in ancient civilization. Rahab saw the earliest days of Israel, and Ruth witnessed its establishment. Bathsheba married David, forerunner of Christ. Matthew is demonstrating a crescendo, building up to the Savior of the world. He finally brings us to Mary, mother of Jesus Himself.

Her story is too complex and wonderful to address it all. I couldn't possibly do justice to the entirety of her role. For our purposes, we will focus on a few parts that inform our identity in Christ, beginning with the fact that she was an early teen when the angel Gabriel announced her selection.

"Do not be afraid, Mary, you have found favor with God. You will be with child and give birth to a son, and you are to give him the name Jesus. He will be great and will be called the Son of the Most High. The Lord God will give him the throne of his father David, and he will reign over the house of Jacob forever; his kingdom will never end."

Let's acknowledge something about God. Most scholars put Mary between thirteen and fifteen years old. That is not in dog years. It isn't a product of ancient fuzzy math. Thirteen in first-century Israel is the same as thirteen today. Someone has to ask it: Was God totally mental? I'm guessing Gabriel showed up in Nazareth thinking, *Is this the wrong address, Almighty? She's just a girl!* This confidence in a young teen is so beyond our modern assessment, it almost seems fabled.

Society has gradually pushed back the age of accountability. Our grandmothers bore ten times the responsibilities ten times earlier than we did. Western culture reshaped the estimation of young people, both their capabilities and time lines. Slowly they've been stripped of value and forced through modern protocol before anyone could possibly take them seriously. Their passion is tempered by adult reason. Their idealism is countered by the status quo. They're just kids, just teenagers, only in their twenties, early thirties. Too young to know, well, anything.

How do we square young Mary with this perspective? Does it address the tension to simply say, "It was a different time, another culture"? Or maybe, "God operates differently now"? Our modern objections include the dangers of being uneducated and inexperienced. Well, according to custom, Mary was nominally educated during her youngest years. She received no formal education and graduated to tending the home. And her experience was limited to Nazareth, described like this by Nathaniel in John's gospel: "Nazareth! Can anything good come from there?" It was hardly a booming metropolis of culture, never even mentioned biblically until Jesus put it on the map.

Mary was not differently qualified than any thirteen-year-old since. The Bible made her humble pedigree clear. She was not a protégé of a great rabbi. There was no special anointing on her as a child. She wasn't identified as a genius or prodigy. She didn't hail from an exceptional family or receive extraordinary advantages. She was a normal thirteen-year-old girl.

And God chose her to bear His Son.

"I BELIEVE IN YOU" — GOD

Let it sink in, believer. No girl is too young, too inexperienced, or too uneducated to be chosen for a holy task. God wrecked a feminine label with each woman in Jesus' family tree. I sense a crescendo, each stereotype intensifying with objections:

- Tamar—too powerless
- Rahab—too tainted
- Ruth—too inferior
- Bathsheba—too broken
- Mary—too young

If God is not affected by those stereotypes, who are we to respond differently? Young woman, God is not waiting for you to grow up before He'll take you seriously. On His calendar, there is no such thing as "Not yet . . . someday." That's nothing but wasted time. Biblically, He engaged believers as young as possible. Joseph, David, Josiah, Daniel, Shadrach/Meshach/Abednego, Uzziah, Jesus, Timothy—all heroes of the Bible, all called as teenagers. God has His eye on the young.

Though compared to Mary I was practically a senior citizen, I wrote my first book at twenty-nine. God and I had some intense conversations about that timing. If age is a disqualifier in secular life, magnify that by a hundred in spiritual circles. I'm too familiar with condescending responses, critical body language, and slightly veiled disdain from my elders. I received the proverbial pat on the head many times: "Oh, you wrote a book! How adorable! That is so sweet, I'm just going to buy a copy for my middle school daughter. She will just love you to pieces!" (To be fair, some of my favorite comments come from senior women when I travel. One in her eighties e-mailed, "You make our Lord proud," and it was so dear, I cried for ten minutes.)

But back to my twenty-nine-year-old self. God gave me such a passion for the study of His Word, I had to write that book. I didn't know everything about studying Scripture—and just a few years later I notice fifty things I'd change or add—but God didn't wait until I was "fully mature" or "more experienced" to issue that assignment. If He had confidence in me, then I wasn't going to argue with His logic.

What about you? Are you caught in the "someday" trap? In your youth, are you just waiting? Maybe you're forty-nine and you're *still* waiting to grow up. Sisters, I'm guessing you're older than thirteen, so enough with the excuses. Or maybe you're thirteen times four, and the "someday" lie has prejudiced you against the next generation. Let's notice the exchange between young Mary and Gabriel.

"I'M SO SURE" — MARY, AGE 13, RESPONSE #1

His announcement surprised her, too. She had a long list of disqualifiers, frankly. Plus, all Israelite women knew that one of them would bear a Savior. That prophecy was passed down every generation. Each pregnant Israelite in David's lineage wondered if she were the chosen one:

> For to us a child is born,
>> to us a son is given,
>> and the government will be on his shoulders.
> And he will be called
>> Wonderful Counselor, Mighty God,
>> Everlasting Father, Prince of Peace.
> Of the increase of his government and peace
>> there will be no end.
> He will reign on David's throne
>> and over his kingdom,
> establishing and upholding it
>> with justice and righteousness
>> from that time on and forever. (Isaiah 9:6-7)

Every mother was aware of the promise, hoping her daughter was the one. Each generation watched expectantly for the Messiah.

So when Mary was chosen, she asked, "How will this be, since I am a virgin?" Let's logically add to her confusion: "since I am a nobody, since I am from nowhere, since I'm just a girl, since there is *no way* I could be the one." This was crazy. This was insane. This was impossible. No one would believe this. Maybe she was hallucinating.

That is *exactly* how it feels to be called before you feel ready. How will this be? Oh, how familiar I am with the obstacles. We don't know enough. No one will listen or believe in us. These are grown-up tasks, and we're junior contributors. We must be hearing God wrong; these assignments couldn't be ours. We'll be instantly discredited by the legitimate ones.

HELP A SISTER OUT

It's all summed up right here:

"The angel answered, 'The Holy Spirit will come upon you, and the power of the Most High will overshadow you. So the holy one to be born will be called the Son of God. Even Elizabeth your relative is going to have a child in her old age, and she who was said to be barren is in her sixth month. For nothing is impossible with God.'"

I'm so in love with His answer. How will this happen, you ask? The power of the Holy Spirit will overshadow you. Even as I type that, relief floods my calling again. In Greek, *power* is the word *dunamis*, from which we derive the word *dynamite*. Daughter, you cannot diminish that kind of force because you're young. I'm sorry, but you're not that powerful. If God wants to activate His dynamite through your young life, you can't stop it. Your call, my call, Mary's call, they originate from the surprising will of God, not our ability to carry them out.

And notice how Gabriel answered her unspoken objection about her age: He referenced Elizabeth, miraculously pregnant in her twilight years. Do you see, ladies? No woman is too young, too old, or too middle-aged to be solicited for God's work. Whether we think a woman is too young to understand the issue, too old to be relevant, or too middle-aged to inspire passion, nothing is impossible with God. Age is a nonfactor, as is a dark history, questionable background, or dubious pedigree.

Elizabeth sets a beautiful example of intergenerational esteem. She didn't balk at God's discernment or lecture Mary endlessly. There were no undercurrents of disrespect. She didn't gossip about this unlikely young mother. Rather, she honored Mary, because clearly God had. "Blessed are you among women, and blessed is the child you will bear! Blessed is she who has believed that what the Lord has said to her will be accomplished!" Precious Elizabeth.

"BRING IT ON" — MARY, AGE 13, RESPONSE #2

Each stage of life holds unique feminine value. Little girls are full of wonder and simple faith. Women in the middle of life have bright lines around their case as they raise the next generation. Empty nesters and seniors are seeded with wisdom; their lives testify to the enduring strength of women.

But I see special qualities in Mary often attributed to youth. I'll point out two.

First, read her response as holy dynamite ignited her young life: "I am the Lord's servant. May it be to me as you have said." A thirteen-year-old virgin from nowhere couldn't possibly bring forth the Savior of the world, but God decided she would, and Mary basically answered, "Bring it on then," a testimony to the optimism of youth. Had she been a bit older, Mary might've responded, "I'm too busy." Older still, maybe, "I'm too tired."

A wonderful characteristic of youth is idealism that adulthood hasn't tarnished. We still have hope for this world. We see challenges and envision solutions. Young women would rather be actively hopeful than resignedly silent. We read God's standards—justice, compassion, a vision for the nations—and say, "Lord, may it be as You have said. I'll be Your girl on the ground."

Disillusionment hasn't set in, and enthusiasm for the kingdom that could be reigns. We've not given up on God, His church, or His dreams, regardless of where they currently stand. Rather than despair, we dream ancient dreams with God, and we hope fresh hopes with Jesus. If He was certain enough to envision it, then we'll be zealous enough to believe that it can happen.

Second, look at Mary's prayer delivered at Elizabeth's house, these two generations ministering to each other, one carrying the forerunner of the other:

My soul glorifies the Lord and my spirit rejoices in God my Savior, for he has been mindful of the humble state of his servant. From now on all generations will call me blessed, for the Mighty One has done great things for me—holy is his name. His mercy extends to those who fear him, from generation to generation. He has performed mighty deeds with his arm; he has scattered those who are proud in their inmost thoughts. He has brought down rulers from their thrones but has lifted up the humble. He has filled the hungry with good things but has sent the rich away empty. He has helped his servant Israel, remembering to be merciful to Abraham and his descendants forever, even as he said to our fathers.

Preach it, girl! Too young, my eye! This prayer indicates considerable knowledge. Not only did Mary borrow lines from Hannah's famous prayer but she nailed the essence of God. Mary wasn't formally educated, but God is not bound by the classroom. Young women are among God's savviest disciples. Don't assume God reveals Himself only to the aged. Just as men once discredited women as receptacles of holy wisdom, we eliminate an entire demographic when we discount today's youth.

FIRST-CENTURY YOUTH ACTIVISM

But it's the wording Mary used that fires me up: The high will be brought low, the proud scattered, the humble lifted up, the rich empty-handed, the poor filled. This is the language of liberation, the transformation of social order and redistribution of resources. Young revolutionaries champion these exact causes today.

Example #1:
Only Jesus would be crazy enough to suggest that if you want to become the greatest, you should become the least. Only Jesus would declare God's blessing on the poor rather than on the rich and would insist that it's not enough to love just your friends. I began to wonder if anybody still believed Jesus meant those things He said. I thought if we just stopped and asked, What if He really meant it? It could turn the world upside-down. It was a shame Christians had become so normal.[2] — Shane Claiborne, 30, *The Irresistible Revolution*

Example #2:
Common Ground is a student-led organization that seeks to improve campus unity by chipping away social barriers,

raising intercultural awareness, improving communication, and taking the initiative on issues related to race, culture and society. This organization emerged entirely as a student initiative and has played a key role in advancing the critical work of racial reconciliation.

Organizations like these—and the students who lead them—offer hope that evangelical Christians in the next generation will build on the best of our piety while extending it into a more consistent practice of Christ-centered service and activism on behalf of a suffering world.[3]—Dr. David Gushee, professor of moral philosophy, Union University, Jackson, Tennessee

Example #3:
Satan, who I believe exists as much as I believe Jesus exists, wants us to believe meaningless things for meaningless reasons. Can you imagine if Christians actually believed that God was trying to rescue us from the pit of our own self-addiction? Can you imagine? Can you imagine what Americans would do if they understood over half the world was living in poverty? Do you think they would change the way they live, the products they purchase, and the politicians they elect? If we believed the right things, the true things, there wouldn't be very many problems on earth.[4]—Donald Miller, 30, *Blue Like Jazz*

Young Christian activism is alive and well, its rhetoric reminiscent of Mary's. I realize that my generation is not the first to envision the end of poverty or genocide or disease or hunger. The church birthed revolutionaries such as Paul of Tarsus, St. Francis, Dirk Willems, Dorothy Day, Martin Luther King Jr., Mother Teresa, and the list goes on. These young people laid the foundation for social revolution and a church driven by the gospel again.

I CAN'T TYPE THIS NEXT SECTION FAST ENOUGH . . .

But what distinguishes our generation is so thrilling, I can hardly breathe. Jeffrey Sachs, brilliant economist and special advisor to United Nations secretary-general Kofi Annan on the millennium development goals, predicted in *The End of Poverty,* "Extreme poverty can be ended not in the time of our grandchildren, but in *our* time. The wealth of the rich world, the power of today's vast storehouses of knowledge, and the declining fraction of the world that needs help to escape from poverty all make the end of poverty a realistic possibility by the year 2025."[5] (Put this book down immediately and buy Jeff's.)

Never has so much wealth been concentrated in the hands of so few. (Let's quickly redefine "wealth": If you make $35,000 annually, you are in the top 4 percent in the world. $50,000 a year? Top 1 percent.) The skills, resources, and opportunities for social revolution are unprecedented. With the extraordinary advantages of global communication and technology, there isn't an international problem that cannot be answered by this generation. We are economically, ecologically, and electronically sophisticated. We are globally organized, positioned for action, and dead serious about social justice and the intersection of the church.

We can do this, girls. We can pull off what Mary envisioned, what her Son began. I imagine a world where ten million children no longer die each year from preventable diseases. We can solve the crisis of starvation — eighteen thousand children will die today from plain old hunger. We could ensure basic water sanitation for the 40 percent of the world who drink wastewater. If God intends His Word to be read, we'd better address the one billion people who cannot sign their name, one-sixth of the global population.

If you are a woman born into wealth (meaning you make more than two dollars a day like half the world) and part of the next generation, I believe you were chosen before the foundation of the earth to be an answer to problems unsolvable until now. This generation was selected for this time—a time so promising and passionate, it has never been rivaled. There is a holy calling awaiting this generation, girls.

We are the ones.

HERE IS THE CHURCH, HERE IS THE STEEPLE

The church reflects the growing passion for Jesus' dream. My friends at LifeWay polled young adults between age eighteen and thirty-five, asking, among other things, "What draws you to a church?" The overwhelming majority responded, "Do they respond to poverty and oppression, or are they silent and self-consumed?"

George Barna, renowned church researcher, predicted in *Revolution,*

> There is a new breed of Christ-follower in America today. These people are Revolutionaries. This groundswell of spiritual passion and intensity is likely to amount to a Third Great Awakening in the United States, but with a very different look, feel, and outcome than previous religious upheavals. In many ways, this new move back to God is designed to return the American Church to its roots—its first century roots, as depicted in Acts 2.[6]

Naysayers dismiss this as the latest church trend, but, if so, it is a very ancient one.

I feel it, sisters. I sense the currents so strongly that my husband and

I left the security of our church to start a new one centered around the marginalized. I'll never forget the day Christ walked me through His conversation with Peter (see John 21), asking me the same questions.

"Jen, do you love Me?"

This seemed aggravating, and I responded a little like Peter did: "Of course I do! Come on, Jesus! Hello? This is *me* you're talking to! If I don't love You, then I should quit this ministry thing and get a job that makes real money. Let's move on to a real topic."

"Feed my lambs."

Hmmm. "I do feed them. I feed them spiritually," I said a little woundedly.

"Jen, do you love Me?"

What *was* this? Was He possibly saying the zillions of hours I minister weren't enough? What was going on here? What was happening? What was this conversation? I expected it to end after my first answer. I said, "Jesus, I *do* love You! Isn't it so obvious? Do You honestly not think I love You? Why are You asking this?"

"Take care of My sheep."

"Don't I?! Do I not care for their souls and nourish them with Your Word? Has my whole life not been spent on Your church?" Now I'm bawling, because I was scared. I sensed that Jesus was about to rock my life. He and I hadn't spoken like this before.

"Jen, do you love Me?"

At this point, I freaked out. I was handling the gospel exactly like I thought I should. I studied it, taught it, wrote about it, breathed it. I constantly counseled, hugged, challenged, and loved women. We'd made so many sacrifices for ministry that I could not wrap my head around this conversation. If these didn't indicate my love for Christ, then I had no idea what to do.

"You're scaring me, Lord. If I am not Your disciple, then nothing is true in the whole world. I love You, and I serve Your people seven days a week. I cannot understand this! What is going on?"

"Feed My sheep."

"I feed their souls."

"Yes, but twenty-four thousand of My sheep will die today because no one fed their hungry bellies. Eighteen thousand of My littlest lambs will die in their mothers' arms today, starved in a world of plenty. My true disciples engage the suffering of the world."

My life changed in that moment. Jesus interrupted my comfortable world of pop-Christianity and enlisted me in the cause of my generation, the mission of His true church. Hunger, poverty, orphans, widows, oppression, war—these are not metaphors in Scripture. As Jesus' brother told us, "What good is it, my brothers, if a man claims to have faith but has no deeds? Can such faith save him? Suppose a brother or sister is without clothes and daily food. If one of you says to him, 'Go, I wish you well; keep warm and well fed,' but does nothing about his physical needs, *what good is it?*" (James 2:14-16, emphasis added).

Jesus said that His gospel was good news for the poor, sick, orphaned, and oppressed because His people would be His hands and feet. What is better news to the starving: a Christian tract, or sustainable agriculture for their village? Which sounds better: a church that prays once a month for the AIDS pandemic, or one that funds clinics and medicine?

We are part of the reason the gospel is good news. If God instructed His millions of followers to care for the poor, and those followers have every resource to do it, then the impoverished have hope. This is the Almighty's plan to alleviate suffering. Help is on its way.

Enter you. Enter me. Enter the church awakening from her violent slumber. Dear ones, how will we answer one day if we fail to intercede? "God, we didn't know"? "We didn't have any resources"? "We were overwhelmed"? "We didn't think You were serious"? The only answer for our generation is to become the hands of Christ. Jesus said, "From the one who has been entrusted with much, much more will be asked" (Luke 12:48).

Let there be no doubt: Our generation has been entrusted with more resources, wealth, opportunities, and knowledge than any before us. God must think highly of our potential. Let's not squander our legacy on self-absorption or chasing the American Dream, a dream the rest of the world cannot afford. But may we hear from our Savior one day: "Whatever you did for one of the least of these brothers of mine, you did for me" (Matthew 25:40).

CHAPTER 11

We Are the Correct Answer

Permission to Be God's Favorite

Truth #5:

Women are favored by God.

LUKE 1

Really, what is special about women? What about us draws the eye of the Lord? (If this is not clear to you yet, turn to chapter 1 and start this book over, and pay attention this time.) Let me offer an adorable character sketch of a woman I knew and shed more light on the goodness of our gender.

My bridal shower was hosted by the ladies at my parents' church. These gals held me in the church nursery, you understand. Most were my mom's friends and my friends' moms. Because my grandpa was a founding deacon in the 1950s, my grandma and her friends were there too, of course. No one would miss the shower for "Larry and Jana's daughter."

As I was practically going into convulsions over napkin rings and bath towels (like I hadn't registered for every single thing), I came to one gift wrapped in a large trash bag. "Ooohh—that's from me!" sang a sweet old voice from the third row.

Lucille Hattabaugh was widowed during World War II and never married again. She taught school for forty years and barely had two dimes to rub together ("poor teacher" is redundant, I know). Lucille was a character, so I knew this would be good. Plus, I heard some promising jingling, guaranteeing some sort of train wreck.

As I lifted the bag, it took about five seconds to figure out what I was seeing. It was a type of chandelier. It had four tiers of . . . something. It was held together with fishing wire. The jingling turned out to be more of a clacking. I looked closer. I squinted. I got it.

It was made entirely of small, plastic Communion cups.

The old girl must have pilfered them for ten years.

"Wow, Ms. Hattabaugh! Look at this! This is, well, this is just, I have never seen anything like this before! This is really something! Whoa, this is really going to go nicely, um, somewhere. Did you make this yourself? You rinsed all these out, right?" No one rescued me, as they were enjoying the chandelier show too much to end it. My girlfriend told me later, "That made the hundred bucks I spent on you totally worth it."

Lucille Hattabaugh was quirky, strange, perhaps just a teeny bit crazy. She clearly had a stealing problem. But here is the grand finale to her story. My mom recently told me that every year, Lucille lived on 25 percent of her meager salary, putting the rest in the offering plate. When she died, it turned out she had systematically saved over twenty-five thousand dollars from her tiny income, and she left every penny to the church, not unlike the poor widow who gave two mites to the temple, drawing the favor of Jesus. I'm sure her mansion in heaven is decorated with diamond chandeliers to replace the Communion-cup versions she settled for on earth.

What is not to love about a woman like that?

Don't you know women make God so proud, when we're not making Him laugh? With our creativity and quirkiness and compassion and courage, we are the daughters of God's dreams. We represent so much goodness. We are devoted mothers and faithful wives, grateful daughters and inseparable sisters. Women are divine. I love you so much, and I didn't even create you.

The feminine trend of self-loathing has robbed us of enjoying God's favor. The self-esteem crisis has reached stunning heights, imposing sanctions on how much we are loved by Christ. It is a tragedy indeed. Imagine if your daughter refused to believe that you loved her, that she had any favor in your eyes. If she wasted away in condemnation and obsessed about past mistakes, resisting the intensity of your love, you would die right along with her spirit.

SWEET CHARITOO

Mary's story gives us hope. As we read it, may we get back in touch with our own favor. While Mary's role in the salvation story was exceptional, there are parallel blessings every woman shares with her. Remember Gabriel's first words to young Mary:

"Greetings, you who are highly favored! The Lord is with you."

The Greek word for *favored* is *charitoo*, meaning "endued with special honor; accepted." Only a fool would deny Mary this special honor. Obviously, being chosen as Christ's mother is a one-time tribute. God saw in her what He wanted for the story. He chooses women for a reason, and that usually includes upending the status quo. Like the others named in Jesus' family tree, Mary had what mattered spiritually and nothing that mattered culturally.

Indeed, Mary was favored, but so are we. Has the Lord not favored each of us with some token of divine love? There is something special about every believer's case. God draws beautiful boundaries around our stories. Some of us were blessed with exceptional gifts, others with exceptional families. Maybe God rescued you from death or gifted you as His extraordinary spokesperson. Some mothers were honored with special children whom only *they* could raise. How often I've seen God grant a daughter the deepest desire of her heart. Perhaps just in the nick of time, Jesus saved you from yourself.

God weaves His Spirit differently through every story. He intersects the lives of His daughters with unique favor. Every woman is crowned with a special honor from Christ. He loves you in a very personal, very individual way. Where and how He stepped into your time line was for you, and only you can tell of it. Make no mistake, you are highly favored. Mary delivered the Son, but the Son delivered you. It is not possible to be more privileged than that.

Sometimes God sweeps majestically into our lives with large motions and life-saving redemption. But He also loves us in quiet, sweet ways, and we fail to notice. "I challenge you to notice the small occurrences in your life," wrote Jacqueline Jakes. "The smell of water, the scent of soap, the cleanliness of your space, the warmth of sunlight, the still of night, the sound of music, the smile of a child, and the millions of events that make this life bearable and blessed."[1]

Stand on a mountain. Breathe the smell of pine trees. Listen to your son sing in the shower. Try to remember the last day you went hungry. God treats us far better than we treat ourselves. I think He makes up ways to bless us sometimes. It's almost embarrassing how much God loves us. Between the treasures He gives away for free— salvation, peace, joy, His voice, unshakeable love, strength, favor—it's a miracle we can contain it all.

God has worked steadily, fervently, and intensely to love us. History is the linear story of God's passion for people. There is nothing He hasn't done to show favor, no end to His efforts. The Law was given as a covenant, not a stumbling block. When it fell short, Jesus forever healed the gap between God and mankind. He made sure His Word was centered on love: His for us, Jesus' for us, ours for each other. Scripture guaranteed that His people would always be loved, by heaven and humanity.

God has screamed it, commanded it, mourned it, restored it, demonstrated it. You are loved, daughter. God systematically orchestrated history for the love of you. In the end, love will be the victor, triumphing over sin, hatred, all that was wrecked on earth. Every movement of God ever was motivated by love. No truth will change your life more than that. You may acknowledge His sovereignty or power. You might get His strength or plans for His kingdom. But until you accept how much He loves you, you really don't know Him at all.

ROUND YON VIRGIN, MOTHER AND CHILD

"The angel said to her, 'Do not be afraid, Mary, you have found favor with God. You will be with child and give birth to a son, and you are to give him the name Jesus. He will be great and will be called the Son of the Most High. The Lord God will give him the throne of his father David, and he will reign over the house of Jacob forever; his kingdom will never end.'"

Favor, indeed. Mary would feel Jesus kicking long before His feet touched the ground. Angels talked to her as she carried Him. Jesus and his cousin John supernaturally communicated from their mothers' wombs: "As soon as the sound of your greeting reached my ears, the baby in my womb leaped for joy," Elizabeth said. This pregnancy was guarded by heaven and stamped with miracles. There was never such a case, before or since.

Yet a spiritual mystery gives us a like privilege: Jesus dwells in us, too. Mary was the physical forerunner of every believer after her. We take the spiritual position where her physical condition left off, because Jesus said before He died,

> I will ask the Father, and he will give you another Counselor to be with you forever—the Spirit of truth. The world cannot accept him, because it neither sees him nor knows him. But you know him, for he lives with you and will be in you. (John 14:16-17)

Charles Spurgeon said, "He lives within us as within a temple, and reigns within us as within a palace. If we be partakers of the Holy Ghost, what more can we desire by way of favor from God, and what greater honor can be bestowed upon us?"[2] All due respect to Mary, but our indwelling of Christ is more powerful than her first one, because it is seeded in victory. Mary carried Jesus when His mission lay ahead. We carry Christ resurrected; the battle is finished. As Matthew Henry noted, "The meanest of those that *follow the Lamb* far excel the greatest of those that went before him" (emphasis added).[3] This isn't because we're superior but because we're covered in Jesus' sacrifice, once and for all.

GETTING ON GOD'S HONOR ROLL OR SOMETHING

It took me years to appreciate the Holy Spirit. I rarely tapped into Him. My experience with the Spirit was restricted to conviction. (Sometimes He makes His presence known with or without our consent.) I lived my life rather parallel to God. I learned about Him, did things for Him, made choices because of Him. There was God, then my life according to God. It was like following rules created by the principal: There was a degree of separation there. God was the leader of my school, and I obeyed in my classroom while He stayed in His office.

I'm not sure exactly how it happened, but I do know where it happened when I finally noticed the Holy Spirit. A few years ago, I decided to study the Word differently. I knew there was more than I was getting, so I abandoned my workbooks and study guides and whatnot and decided to go it alone. Except I discovered I wasn't alone. The Word was the matchmaker that connected me and the Spirit.

It was like reading the Bible for the first time. My dormant relationship with the Spirit was activated, and everything changed. It began in the Word, but once I figured out how He speaks to me, the volume stayed permanently up. He intersected my life everywhere: in prayer, in relationships, in all parts of life. He wins us over where we listen best. I'm a Bible student. That is my thing, so that's where He pursued me. You may hear Him in nature first, or maybe through music. His voice might become familiar through prayer or dreams. He knows how to get your attention.

As the Spirit speaks, I've never been more aware of my own favor. There is no greater delight than this intimacy. How we've lost the thrill of His internal presence. After Jesus' resurrection, two things were different: We had salvation through Christ, and we had the Holy Spirit. How have we forgotten this treasure? We bear as close a relationship to Christ as the virgin mother did; His presence is as real in our hearts as it was in her womb.

Favored, favored, favored is the New Testament daughter of Christ. You are not obligated to a Law that "made nothing perfect" (Hebrews 7:19). You are not a predecessor of Jesus, stripped of your feminine value. You are not dependent on angels or prophets to deliver God's messages. You are not an outsider looking into God's chosen nation. You are not awaiting the promised Messiah who would change everything.

Not you.

With the arrival of Jesus, the Messiah, that fateful dilemma is resolved. Those who enter into Christ's being-here-for-us no longer have to live under a continuous, low-lying black cloud. A new power is in operation. The Spirit of life in Christ, like a strong wind, has magnificently cleared the air, freeing you from a fated lifetime of brutal tyranny at the hands of sin and death. (Romans 8:1-2, MSG)

Give me one day this side of the Cross than ten thousand before it.

Receive that, dear one, you who are highly favored! The Lord is with you, too.

"DEAR TEXAS, I LOVE YOU A LOT" — GOD

Speaking of highly favored, it's time to talk about Texas. If you are from here or ever passed through, the following is common knowledge. Texans are the most (self-proclaimed) geographically superior people on the planet. We feel bad for those born in inferior states (meaning the other forty-nine). No one loves Texas more than Texas. If possible, Texas would mate with itself and spawn a pure race of little Texases.

We plaster Texas stars on every surface from Dallas to Houston, Abilene to Tyler. They are chiseled into our buildings, painted on our street art, engraved in our highways, and tattooed on our bodies. When my friend Mark drove to Austin from Oklahoma, he said, "If I see one more star on one more thing, I'm driving my car into oncoming traffic." (A Texan would never do that, of course. We're excellent drivers.)

Bumper stickers you'll see with alarming frequency here:

- Texas: It's bigger than France
- American by birth, Texan by the grace of God
- Life is too short not to live it as a Texan

My children, educated in this state since birth, cannot recite one fact about a world war or international leader, but they learned to sing "The Eyes of Texas" in kindergarten. They may not be able to enter an intelligent discussion someday, but they can sure as heck sing the right words at a Longhorn game. My five-year-old tells people he lives in the country of Texas, as do our senators.

This is our eighth year in Austin, and I've only once heard a disparaging word against our beloved city. Some college boys were painting our house while another crew was redoing our floors. During a break, one of the floor guys said he was new to Austin. We assumed, of course, he'd fallen under its spell and asked if he loved it. He said, "No, it's like the armpit of Texas here."

There was no sound in the room. No one breathed or moved for five seconds.

Finally, one of the University of Texas boys said, "Dude, do you want us to take you out back right now? We will fight you." I feared for his life and urged him to take it back. *Take it back, man!* He went back to work as though we were a bunch of overzealous patriot freaks or something, while we held hands and prayed that his ignorant blasphemy would not bring a curse on our home.

I'm just saying, you cannot drive through, fly over, boat past, or step foot in Texas without immediately understanding the depth of its pride. It's too strong for humility, too intense for subtlety. It is in-your-face obvious; sorry if it makes you throw up in your mouth a little.

JESUS' HOMEGIRLS

I believe that women are like God's Texas (redundant). We bear His image so obviously. It is abundantly clear He is in love with us. Just look at us: Our presence practically shouts His mercy, oozes His tenderness. God placed women in every nook and cranny of the universe, declaring

His majesty. There is nothing subtle about our design; we were created to bring God glory, and we do. I imagine onlookers saying, "Sheesh! God is so obsessed with women! We get it, God—You love them!"

It's tempting to view the objectification of women and assume God is more concerned with men, less involved with women. But no man ever liberated women like Jesus did. His interaction with the undervalued female population revolutionized our position. With Him, there was no double standard, no exclusion, and no limits on women's God-given destinies.

Dorothy Sayers addressed it perfectly:

Perhaps it is no wonder that the women were first at the Cradle and last at the Cross. They had never known a man like this Man—there never has been such another. A prophet and teacher who never nagged at them, never flattered or coaxed or patronized; who never made arch jokes about them, never treated them as "The women, God help us!" or "The ladies, God bless them!"; who rebuked without querulousness and praised without condescension; who took their questions and arguments seriously; who never mapped out their sphere for them, never urged them to be feminine or jeered at them for being female; who had no axe to grind and no uneasy male dignity to defend; who took them as he found them and was completely unselfconscious. There is no act, no sermon, no parable in the whole Gospel that borrows its pungency from female perversity; nobody could possibly guess from the words and deeds of Jesus that there was anything "funny" about woman's nature.[4]

The respect Jesus gave women drew much male criticism. "What is *with* Jesus and women? What is His *deal* with them?" they surely asked. His disciples couldn't deny Jesus' affinity for women, though they didn't understand it yet. It was so obvious, like a Texas star on every last surface, impossible to miss.

It still is.

I cannot count how often I've watched a girlfriend execute her talents or display Jesus' mercy and I want to give God a standing ovation. Where would this earth be without us? How much less of God would we know if women weren't reflecting half His image so well?

Enough with the self-deprecation. Enough with the whiny Jesus-couldn't-love-me drama. That is so over-the-top ridiculous, Jesus would be rolling over in His grave (were He still there). God could not communicate His favor clearer if He mowed the message into our front yards every morning, like a crop circle. We have no right to minimize His love through a poor self-image. We do not get to dictate His affection. No sin, no defect, no character flaw is more potent than the love of Christ. If the Cross were dependent on the merits of humanity, it would've been obsolete the same day Jesus hung on it.

Jesus loves you because He does.

Jesus set you free because He wanted to.

Jesus values you because you have value.

Mary birthed Jesus in a humble manger, void of any traditional honor. My affection for Him tempts me to envision a grander entrance, worthy of this Star of Bethlehem. I'd like Jesus to get the respect He deserved. But laid in a manger, God extended an invitation for *anyone* to come to Him. We might tremble approaching a throne but cannot fear a manger.

Charles Spurgeon said,

Never could there be a being more approachable than Christ. No rough guards pushed poor petitioners away; no array of officious friends were allowed to keep off the importunate widow or the man who clamored that his son might be made whole; the hem of his garment was always trailing where sick folk could reach it, and he himself had a hand always ready to touch the disease, an ear to catch the faintest accents of misery, a soul going forth everywhere in rays of mercy, even as the light of the sun streams on every side beyond that orb itself.

Come to him, ye that are weary and heavy-laden! Come to him, ye that are broken in spirit, ye who are bowed down in soul! Come to him, ye that despise yourselves and are despised of others! Come to him, publican and harlot! Come to him, thief and drunkard! In the manger there he lies, unguarded from your touch and unshielded from your gaze. Bow the knee, and kiss the Son of God; accept him as your Savior, for he puts himself into that manger that you may approach him. The throne of Solomon might awe you, but the manger of the Son of David must invite you.[5]

Come, you who are highly favored.

CHAPTER 12

Proofs and Statistics

How Sisters Are Changing the World

I'd like to nominate my girlfriends and me for the Mother of the Year award. (When *do* they pass that thing out?) We all have seven-year-old daughters, so we're living parallel lives of *That's So Raven*, *High School Musical I* and *II*, and *Hannah Montana*. Our sweet, chubby preschoolers somehow turned into skinny, dramatic Valley girls. None of us knows how this happened. My daughter, Sydney, actually said of a friend's outfit, "Adorable! That's *so* Limited Too!"—a store I've never bought even one item from.

Anyway, we can't seem to stop this, so when we heard that The Cheetah Girls were coming to Austin, the moms mobilized. (If you have no idea what I'm talking about, you obviously don't have a daughter between the ages of six and sixteen.) I asked our close friends if we could use their box at the Irwin Center arena for the concert, if they weren't going. Because their kids were grown, they had no clue who The Cheetah Girls were ("Is it an animal act?") and graciously offered their box.

Six of us told our daughters we were having a Girls Night Out, dinner and a movie. Just for fun, we suggested, let's all dress in chee-tah clothes. We went to Fran's, the best dive in Austin for burgers and shakes, and gathered our daughters in one booth. Then out came the video cameras:

"Hey, girls, are you having fun so far?"

"Yeeeaaaahhhhh!!!"

"We have something special to tell you . . ."

"What? What?" the tweens hollered.

"We're not actually going to a movie tonight."

"What?! Why?! I TOTALLY wanted to see *Happily N'Ever After!*"

"Because we're going to THE CHEETAH GIRLS CONCERT!"

(Insert mass, utter pandemonium here.) All twelve of us were jumping up and down, looking like a white-trash convention in our cheetah clothes. At this point, everyone in the restaurant was clap-ping, thrilled for this show they just got for free. We whisked the girls to the arena, where they saw their first concert from box seats with a private bathroom.

The arena was filled with thousands of moms and daughters and a few brave Cheetah Daddies (one whose identity we promised to pro-tect, so I'll only say his initials are "Guy Clayton.") We danced and sang (we knew every word) and waved our glow sticks. We jumped and laughed. "Let me hear my Cheetah Mommas!" "Wooooo-hoooooo!" yelled us CMs. We took our happy, exhausted, glowing daughters home at midnight. Sydney told me as I tucked her in bed,

"Thank you, Mama. You changed my life!"

Admittedly, the Cheetah Girls concert will probably not alter her life's trajectory, but it felt like it to her. At seven, she thought I'd given her the best gift of her life, and she was convinced she'd never be the same.

It is with the greatest pleasure I share some stories of women legitimately improving lives. They are affecting the world, and it will never be the same for their touch. The women and men and children they serve will all sincerely say, "Thank you. You changed my whole life."

I've decided to highlight women exclusively from my circle. Not because we're the best women on earth or there is nothing better going on anywhere else. My aim is to demonstrate the power of women on a micro-scale. I could select the headliners you've heard of, but I hope you'll see what God is doing with the normal, everyday women of the world. Even more, I hope you'll catch a vision for what God could do with you, daughter of Christ. If He can use my friends and me, trust me, He can use you and yours. We represent normal women everywhere. So allow me to introduce some friends who embody the spirit of femininity and use it to heal the world.

ORPHAN LOVER

My Girlfriend Caroline Boudreaux was a hard-hitting executive with Fox when she decided she hated her job. Stuck in endless Austin traffic, in a suit and high heels, with an irate client screaming at her on the phone, she decided she was done. In 1999, at age thirty, she quit to travel the world for one year with her friend. Their goal was to enjoy summer for a year, moving wherever summer was happening.

Her friend asked if they could stop in India. Evidently, she had sponsored a child for several years, and she wanted to see if he really existed. One poor boy in a country of a billion? Shouldn't be hard. Sure enough, they found him and decided to stay for three weeks after a ceremonial village welcome.

One night the director of the Christian Children's Fund there invited them to dinner at his house. Caroline was met by a hundred smiling but severely malnourished children, all shaved bald. She had never thought about orphans, much less spent time with any, but Caroline and her friend stayed the whole day.

Caroline said, "Later that evening, a little girl, Sheebani, put her head on my knee. She was so tired. I picked her up, and she pushed her body into mine. I sang her a lullaby and rocked her to sleep. I went upstairs to find her crib and found thirty wooden slatted beds. No pillows, no mattresses, no blankets, just wooden slats similar to a picnic table. It was chilling and incomprehensible. When I heard her bones hit that wooden bed, I broke. I couldn't believe she lived this way. I knew I had to do something to help her. I had to act."

Caroline came home and launched The Miracle Foundation with her life savings, birthed that evening in India. Initially, she planned to open an international adoption agency and rescue children from those deplorable conditions. She soon discovered that international adoption plus India equals red tape and corruption. (In 2006, out of twenty-five million orphans, only 2,479 were adopted domestically and 853 internationally.) With a thousand dollars to her name, she met with Alan Graham, a saint in Austin who organized Mobile Loaves and Fishes, which feeds thousands of homeless each year.

From that meeting of two kingdom visionaries, Caroline shifted her nonprofit from an adoption agency to a sponsorship program, supporting the millions of unadoptable children in India. Her mission is so amazing. The Miracle Foundation has absorbed and renovated five orphanages, creating an environment these children never dreamed of, plus sponsoring every child.

More exciting are Caroline's Ideal Villages—orphanages built from scratch, arranged like a family environment, beautiful enough to vacation at. The foundation has two on the ground already. When children leave Caroline's orphanages, they are educated, bilingual, computer-literate, healthy, loved, and, most important, eligible for college and marriage—the two elevators out of poverty.

I wish you could know Caroline. I've left a thousand details out of her amazing story. (She was recently commissioned to design a database for all of India's orphans. I had to throw that in.) But she is literally the hands of Christ to these forsaken children. She was working a regular nine-to-five just eight years ago, and now she meets with the Honorable Minister for Women and Child Welfare and gives a future to thousands of Indian orphans.

Yes, she is tall and gorgeous and completely charismatic, but she's not terribly different from any of us. She was a normal subscriber to the American Dream when God interrupted her comfort, and she simply obeyed, centering her life around a basic tenet of the gospel: "Religion that God our Father accepts as pure and faultless is this: to look after orphans and widows in their distress and to keep oneself from being polluted by the world" (James 1:27). She had no idea what she was doing. It wasn't all figured out. In fact, when I sat in her Sixth Street office deciding how to partner with her, I said, "I'm sure you have a protocol that I stepped right around or something." She said, "Are you kidding me? We write our script every day."

I am so proud to know her. I am passionate about her ministry; don't get me started on it unless you have thirty minutes to listen to my ravings. Go immediately to her website at www.miraclefoundation.org and meet her. Send her money. Sponsor an orphan. Go with her to India and see for yourself. Caroline Boudreaux — innovative, determined, resourceful, compassionate. I want to be just like her when I grow up.

MAKEUP MISSIONARY AND SKIN CARE SERVANT

Jessica Thompson and I went to college together, back when she was Jessica Bender and I was Jen King. As girls at our Baptist college tended to do, we married pastors and went into full-time ministry.

She and her husband and their four kids serve at P. Here is Jessica's story, in her words:

> The movie *Hotel Rwanda* awakened many of us to the unimaginable tragedy that occurred in Rwanda in 1994. Five years ago, my husband and I experienced firsthand the emotional and physical scars that genocide left behind. With more than one million men, women, and children murdered in one hundred days, you can imagine the stories we encountered during our trip to Rwanda.
>
> There was one woman who will forever stand out. Her name is Gaudence. Gaudence was the most joy-filled person I'd ever met in my life. She was magnetic. I was especially impressed with her joy, realizing she owned only the clothes on her back. Little did I know . . .
>
> On the last day in Kigali, I said a tearful good-bye to her. As Gaudence walked away from our van, the translator told me Gaudence's whole story. During the genocide, Gaudence awoke one night to her bedroom filled with armed soldiers. They had already murdered her husband and two of her children, then gang-raped her and left her for dead. But she did not die. In fact, she lived to not only care for her two surviving children but also two other orphans who lost their parents in the genocide.
>
> If you met Gaudence, you would never guess that this horrible tragedy was part of her past. Her name truly embodies her joyful life attitude: GO DANCE! As we left Rwanda to return to our comfortable home, I was convicted to help these people. I couldn't get the faces of three hundred thousand orphans and fifty-five thousand women fighting AIDS out of my mind. But every time I thought about it,

I faced the roadblock of finances. (Being married to a pastor with four children has always called for creativity in that realm.)

One day I decided that money would no longer stand in my way. I started my own business to send money to the nonprofit organizations doing incredible work in Rwanda. Not only was I blessed with success, I was given countless opportunities to share Gaudence's story with thousands of people.

Let me tell you specifically what she did: At age twenty-nine, Jessica started selling Arbonne, and she rose through the ranks so quickly, she was driving an Arbonne Mercedes-Benz in six months. But, more important, she ships her profits to Global Action (www.global-act.org), a nonprofit that supports local relief efforts already on the ground in Rwanda.

Starting a business to give money away draws attention. Jessica was chosen as one of three women out of sixteen thousand consultants to share her story at the Arbonne National Training Celebration in 2006. At that point, Gaudence was unaware that Jessica even knew her history (the translator relayed it), much less how Jessica was sending relief money, telling her story to conventions and reporters and anyone who would listen. Hardly anyone in Rwanda knows Gaudence's name, but thousands of Americans do now.

Jessica traveled back to Rwanda earlier this year, and through divine intervention, she and Gaudence reconnected. (Armed with nothing but Gaudence's picture and first name, Jessica had no idea how to find her. While standing in the Dallas airport, Africa bound, she turned and three feet away was the translator who had told Gaudence's story five years earlier. She gave Jessica the numbers to find Gaudence once she landed.)

With great joy, Jessica told Gaudence how far her story reached. They cried and hugged and held hands, sisters across nations and the chasm of poverty. Gaudence prayed over Jessica before she left. We don't know what she said, but prayer is the language of heaven. In addition to Global Action, Jessica now sends $150 a month directly to Gaudence—almost eight times what Gaudence makes cultivating other people's land for seventy cents a day. She can now feed the five hungry children who depend on her. Jessica Thompson—merciful, selfless, imaginative, loving. Well done, good and faithful servant of the Most High.

WHITE GIRL WITH A BIG HEART

My Girlfriend Anna Melvin is "blessed" with a burden for the Arab world, population 320 million. God gave her a deep desire to bring the hope of Jesus to this oppressed, closed region. She gobbled down book after book on Muslim women. She enrolled in Perspectives, a fifteen-session course to mobilize Christ followers around God's global purposes. After leading a prayer team for months—interceding for countries and regions individually—Anna traveled to North Africa for an international women's conference supported by Global Action (www.global-act.org).

The American women did not go to organize, administrate, or teach, like we usually do. This was an underground Christian conference for Arab women by Arab women. The American team had one objective: Love those women. We don't understand the oppression that Christian women endure in that region. Many an Arab woman came as the only believer in her village. They are isolated and persecuted, with little opportunity for Christian fellowship. They hold secret meetings under the threat of imprisonment or worse, so much do they love their God.

Anna gave me permission to tell one woman's story, one of the first Algerian believers. For her safety, I will call her "R"; her real name means "merciful," which you'll appreciate in thirty seconds. In her older years, R came to Christ, but her husband did not. She wanted to hold Christian meetings in her home but feared that her husband would turn them in. So R prayed, "God, you have to prevent my husband from discovering what we are doing. I am going to open my home for these Bible studies, and you have to work on my husband so we won't get exposed."

She prayed this prayer with faith, believing that God could do it, and He answered with a miracle. Each week for eight years of Christian meetings, the Lord made her husband deaf and paralyzed—just during her Bible study. When the last believer walks out her door, he comes out of it. He'll say, "I've been calling you! I couldn't move! Why didn't you come help me?" And R says, "I did call back to you, but you were deaf and couldn't hear me. I couldn't come that second, but I am here to help you now." This has happened every week for eight years as God protects this little flock.

Don't imagine that God doesn't still perform miracles.

My sweet friend basically forced her way into the hearts of the Arab women there. Suspicious and skeptical of the Americans, the Arab women had no idea what to do with this young white girl who would not quit smiling and touching them. She won them over, as she does everyone. By the end of the conference, they were worshipping together in their native languages, sisters in Christ.

Anna said,

When I read how God loves the lonely, the oppressed, the aching, the forsaken, the suffering, I think of these women. They are lonely, and I can be their friend. They feel unloved, as if their value in life is limited. I can love them and affirm their value in God's eyes. They are hurting; I can listen. They are oppressed, and although I can't change that, I can make them feel human and cared for. They are forgotten about. I can remember them in my prayers. This is at the root of my passion for the Arab World.

Anna is taking two teams of women back this year with the sole purpose of loving these brave disciples of Christ in a region that despises Him. Anna Melvin — tender, faithful, courageous, determined. You truly make our Lord proud.

FROM ONE TO FOUR (A BIG WAL-MART BILL)

My Girlfriend Andrea Hill and I have been tight since eighth grade. I was the pushy girl who invited everyone to church; she was the one who finally came. Bam! Friends forever. (Side note: Andrea is the ultimate athlete, not one ounce of froufrou. Naturally, her daughter's life ambition is to be a cheerleader/dancer. At six, when making a wish under the St. Louis arch, her little girl said passionately, "I wish my mom had better fashion.")

Andrea and her husband, Michael, are teachers in a small Kansas town. They agreed to have one biological child, then embrace the dream God put in her heart as a young girl: adoption. She said,

> Throughout our teaching careers, we saw kids who needed a parent figure, someone to care about them, to invest in their lives, and even though we did that at school, it fell short of making a long-term difference. Michael and I felt that the Lord placed this on our hearts and gave us more love to give. We could talk all day about what needed to be done, but what good was that? God wanted action from us, and I don't believe we would have peace if we did nothing. The most profound impact we could make was to adopt a child taken out of his home and raise him with Christ's love.

To that end, they entered the foster-care system to answer both convictions: (1) adopt a child (2) in an abusive or neglected situation. At age thirty-two, barely entered in the foster-care database, Andrea got the call: "We have two-year-old twin girls and their three-year-old brother. Their mother pours a box of cereal on the floor for them to eat that week. Do you want all three?"

Andrea didn't even hesitate. She went instantly from a mother of one to four, making a mad dash to Wal-Mart to stock up on diapers, clothes, food, bedding, and toys that day. The kids came to her malnourished, underdeveloped, and paranoid. Her son would wet his pants rather than get up from the table, fearing the food would be gone when he got back. Oh, you should see them now. Beautiful, healthy, eyes full of light. The kids have different fathers, and when we met them this summer, my daughter said, "I really like those twin girls with the brown brother." Who doesn't?

When the kids came up for adoption, Andrea and Mike immediately began the process. They are now fighting tooth and nail to become permanent parents for these three children. Sure, they had one child in mind when they started this adventure, but God had three destined for the last name "Hill": three beautiful children who will never remember the neglect they suffered and will never forget the unconditional love they've been given.

Andrea said, "Most people thought or still think we are crazy. Take on three additional kids?! Wouldn't we have to sacrifice? Give up stuff? Live very 'cozy' in our little home? But every argument just made us laugh. God didn't say it would make sense to other people. The blessings have been more than my heart can express." Andrea Hill—obedient, merciful, sacrificial, amazing. You are worthy of every good blessing in the universe, dear friend.

SO MUCH TO CELEBRATE

One more. If ever I was pressed to name a mentor family, I'd choose the Steve and Norma Murphy clan of Tulsa. At our first church position, their two youngest daughters were in our youth group. (Of their two oldest daughters, one was my age and one was Brandon's age. So we were basically like their kids. God bless you, Murphys, for acting as if you took us seriously.)

By 2001, Norma's four daughters had crossed the college graduation platform and left her house. At age fifty-one, rather than kicking her feet up for a well-deserved break, Norma went a different direction. It began with the decision to bring her cousin, struggling with addiction, to Tulsa, where they could help her. Frustrated with secular recovery options, Norma's pastor, Hess Hester, suggested Celebrate Recovery, then a little-known Christian program out of Rick Warren's Saddleback Church.

Because Norma had no idea what it was, she went to the annual CR Summit at Saddleback with her cousin, hoping to "help her." What she realized was that she, too, needed recovery—not from addiction but from control and anger in her marriage.

Norma came home changed. She had a new assignment. At Southern Hills Baptist Church, she became the ministry leader of the first Celebrate Recovery program in Oklahoma, starting with thirty people ready to deal with their hurts, habits, and hang-ups. Not only did she lead CR, but she and Steve worked the twelve steps too, allowing God to bring healing and lasting change into their marriage.

As Celebrate Recovery grew nationally, Norma became the Oklahoma state representative for the program. From the first one she started, there are now more than thirty CR branches in Oklahoma. She even accepted the position of National Assimilation Coach for a season. At Southern Hills, 220 people have completed the steps, 125 are working them now, and over 120 people serve this ministry weekly. Norma has seen people freed from every addiction, compulsion, and dysfunction.

When Hess Hester, her pastor, asked how to further support CR (don't *ever* ask Norma a question like that unless you're serious), she told him, "Work the steps yourself." So healing was the program for him, their chapter began a pastors' recovery group with local ministers, the first one ever. When John Baker, the founder of CR, heard about it, he asked Hess to speak at the annual CR Summit and has since created a national Celebrate Pastors Recovery program.

I wish you could see Norma. She is this tiny, blonde, soft-spoken angel; it almost masks the fire in her belly for recovery, but not quite. "What fuels my passion is seeing lives totally transformed, starting in our marriage," said Norma. "Celebrate Recovery is a new way of thinking." Read her testimony at http://www.shbc-tulsa.org/cr/norma .html and fall madly in love with her. Better yet, check out Celebrate. Recovery at www.celebraterecovery.com and fall madly in love with God's healing power. Norma Murphy—humble, determined, brave, compassionate. May every woman in my generation have a mentor like her.

GETTING IT DONE

"Such a large crowd of witnesses is all around us! So we must get rid of everything that slows us down, especially the sin that just won't let go. And we must be determined to run the race that is ahead of us" (Hebrews 12:1, CEV). Indeed, these women jolt me out of dangerous complacency with their passion and obedience. I am so proud to call them friends. Their faith has long abandoned the trend of Christian consumerism.

Charles Spurgeon preached in 1886,

It is horrible to be living to be saved, living to get to heaven, living to enjoy religion, and yet never to live to bless others, and ease the misery of a moaning world. Do you not know that it is all nonsense to regard religion as a selfish spiritual trade by which we save our own souls? It is useless to hope for peace till you know how to love. Unless your religion tears you away from yourself, and makes you live for something nobler than even your own spiritual good, you have not passed out of the darkness into the light of God.[1]

Just when discouragement starts to set in regarding a church asleep at the wheel, I see the Carolines, Jessicas, Annas, Andreas, and Normas of the world getting it done. I'll confess that I wanted this book to be all about social and religious revolution and the plight of the world (see my next project), but God insisted on addressing the feminine identity crisis. "Honestly, God, does the world need another book on identity? Isn't this already covered?"

God squashed my dissention with one soft answer: "Only spiritually healthy women will change the world. Work on the first, and you'll become the second." I was immediately won over, because He's right. When women are trapped in fear and self-loathing and guilt and confusion, all their energy is spent on themselves. It becomes a vicious cycle of distraction wasting years of our lives. Women will not be released into their gifts while they're spiraling in an identity crisis.

The spiritually secure woman is free to love others. She is liberated to exercise her talents and bring healing to this world. She does not spend all her time rehashing her misery or passively waiting for everyone else to change. Choose to rise above the rubble of insecurity and watch what God will do with your precious life. I doubt very seriously that Mother Teresa spent her days worrying about her weight and lamenting what a wretch she was. What a waste of energy for the blessed daughters of the King!

It is time.

It's time to move forward in strength. It is time to declare a cease-fire with men and partner with them once again. It's time to reclaim our fierce intelligence. Don't go another day without receiving the forgiveness that's already on the table. Let's tap into our feminine courage and abandon our prejudices. Today is the day to celebrate our beauty and leverage our heartaches for growth. Now is the time to unleash the power of our influence and take up the banner for our generation. It's time to saturate others with healing, wisdom, and love. Let's immediately receive God's tender favor, reserved for His daughters.

It is time to give Jesus what He paid for: you. Whole, beautiful, healthy you. He'll fight for your honor and defend your cause. You just be. You just be the amazing, stunning woman you are. Celebrate your femininity. Enjoy it. Embrace every wonderful facet God instilled in you. Cherish all that is divine about being a girl, and then tilt your face toward heaven and bless the One who created you, treasured one. You are wonderful and beloved; God adores you. The end.

Fear not, for I have redeemed you;
I have summoned you by name; you are mine. (Isaiah 43:1)

Notes

CHAPTER 1: THE IRRATIONAL EQUATION OF FEMININITY

1. Loren Cunningham and David Joel Hamilton, *Why Not Women? A Fresh Look at Scripture on Women in Missions, Ministry, and Leadership* (Seattle: YWAM Publishing, 2000), 77, 83.
2. Cunningham and Hamilton, 90.
3. Laura Bobak, "For Sale: The Innocence of Cambodia," *Ottawa Sun*, October 24, 1996.
4. Lisa Bevere, *Fight Like a Girl: The Power of Being a Woman* (New York: Warner Faith, 2006), 103.
5. Jo Freeman, "The Women's Liberation Movement: Its Origins, Structures, and Ideas," www.cwluherstory.com/CWLUArchive/histwom.html.
6. Bevere, 124.

CHAPTER 2: GREATER THAN, LESS THAN, OR EQUAL

1. John and Stasi Eldredge, *Captivating: Unveiling the Mystery of a Woman's Soul* (Nashville: Nelson, 2005), 86.
2. Lisa Bevere, *Fight Like a Girl: The Power of Being a Woman* (New York: Warner Faith, 2006), 30.
3. Bevere, 49.

4. Jacqueline Jakes, *God's Trophy Women: You Are Blessed and Highly Favored* (New York: Warner Faith, 2006), 2, 4–5.

5. Dr. Henry Cloud and Dr. John Townsend, *Boundaries: When to Say Yes, When to Say No, to Take Control of Your Life* (Grand Rapids, MI: Zondervan, 1992), 134–135.

CHAPTER 3: THE ART OF CALCULATION

1. Celia Rivenbark, *Stop Dressing Your Six-Year-Old Like a Skank: A Slightly Tarnished Southern Belle's Words of Wisdom* (New York: St. Martin's Press, 2006), 29.

2. Lisa Bevere, *Fight Like a Girl: The Power of Being a Woman* (New York: Warner Faith, 2006), 31.

3. Michelle McKinney Hammond, *The Power of Being a Woman: Embracing the Triumph of the Feminine Spirit* (Eugene, OR: Harvest House, 2004), 64.

4. Clayborne Carson and Kris Shepard, eds., *A Call to Conscience: The Landmark Speeches of Dr. Martin Luther King, Jr.* (New York: Warner Books, 2001), 32.

5. Shane Claiborne, *The Irresistible Revolution: Living as an Ordinary Radical* (Grand Rapids, MI: Zondervan, 2006), 65.

6. Carson and Shepard, 53.

CHAPTER 4: A BUNCH OF REDUCED FRACTIONS

1. *The NIV Study Bible* (Grand Rapids, MI: Zondervan, 2002), 286.

2. En.wikipedia.org/wiki/kanab.

3. Bible.cc/Joshua/2-13.htm.

4. Charles Spurgeon, "Rahab's Faith," *The Spurgeon Archive*, March 1, 1857, www.spurgeon.org/sermons/0119.htm.

5. Shane Claiborne, *The Irresistible Revolution: Living as an*

Ordinary Radical (Grand Rapids, MI: Zondervan, 2006), 262–263.

6. Donald Miller, *Blue Like Jazz: Nonreligious Thoughts on Christian Spirituality* (Nashville: Nelson, 2003), 79.

CHAPTER 5: EXPONENTIATION

1. Lisa Bevere, *Fight Like a Girl: The Power of Being a Woman* (New York: Warner Faith, 2006), 19.

2. Shane Claiborne, *The Irresistible Revolution: Living as an Ordinary Radical* (Grand Rapids, MI: Zondervan, 2006), 204–205.

CHAPTER 6: INCONGRUENT SEGMENTS

1. Tony Campolo, *Speaking My Mind: The Radical Evangelical Prophet Tackles the Tough Issues Christians Are Afraid to Face* (Nashville: W Publishing, 2004), 153–154.

2. Shane Claiborne, *The Irresistible Revolution: Living as an Ordinary Radical* (Grand Rapids, MI: Zondervan, 2006), 221.

3. Campolo, 155.

CHAPTER 7: FEMININE DIMENSIONS

1. John and Stasi Eldredge, *Captivating: Unveiling the Mystery of a Woman's Soul* (Nashville: Nelson, 2005), 132.

2. http://heartquotes.net/Beauty.html.

3. Michelle McKinney Hammond, *The Power of Being a Woman: Embracing the Triumph of the Feminine Spirit* (Eugene, OR: Harvest House, 2004), 36.

4. Ralph Ellison, in *The Quote Garden*, www.quotegarden.com/beauty.html.

5. Ralph Waldo Emerson, in *The Quote Garden*, www.quotegarden .com/beauty.html.

6. Ville Valo, in *The Quote Garden*, www.quotegarden.com/beauty .html.

7. www.kennedy-center.org/about/virtual_tour/jkf-quotes.html.

8. Loren Cunningham and David Joel Hamilton, *Why Not Women? A Fresh Look at Scripture on Women in Missions, Ministry, and Leadership* (Seattle: YWAM Publishing, 2000), 102–103.

CHAPTER 8: PAINFUL SUBTRACTION

1. Jacqueline Jakes, *God's Trophy Women: You Are Blessed and Highly Favored* (New York: Warner Faith, 2006), 5–6.

CHAPTER 9: THE THEORY OF MULTIPLICATION

1. www.usatoday.com/news/world/2007-02-17-un-hunger_x.htm.

2. Lisa Bevere, *Fight Like a Girl: The Power of Being a Woman* (New York: Warner Faith, 2006), 37.

3. John and Stasi Eldredge, *Captivating: Unveiling the Mystery of a Woman's Soul* (Nashville: Nelson, 2005), 204–205.

4. Eldredge, 149.

5. Michelle McKinney Hammond, *The Power of Being a Woman: Embracing the Triumph of the Feminine Spirit* (Eugene, OR: Harvest House, 2004), 217.

6. Robert F. Kennedy, address of the Day of Affirmation: "It Is from the Numberless," University of Capetown, South Africa, June 6, 1966.

CHAPTER 10: ROUNDING DOWN

1. www.businessweek.com/magazine/content/06-12/b3976001 .htm.

2. Shane Claiborne, *The Irresistible Revolution: Living as an Ordinary Radical* (Grand Rapids, MI: Zondervan, 2006), 40–41.

3. David Gushee, "For Next Generation of Christian Activists, Evangelism Is Not Enough," *Associated Baptist Press*, opinion section, February 22, 2007, www.abpnews.com/1765.article.

4. Donald Miller, *Blue Like Jazz: Nonreligious Thoughts on Christian Spirituality* (Nashville: Nelson, 2003), 106–107.

5. Jeffrey D. Sachs, *The End of Poverty: Economic Possibilities for Our Time* (New York: Penguin Books, 2005), 3.

6. George Barna, *Revolution*, www.barna.org/FlexPage .aspx?Page=Resource&ResourceID=196.

CHAPTER 11: WE ARE THE CORRECT ANSWER

1. Jacqueline Jakes, *God's Trophy Women: You Are Blessed and Highly Favored* (New York: Warner Faith, 2006), 190.

2. Charles Spurgeon, "The Key-Note of a Choice Sonnet," *The Spurgeon Archive*, www.spurgeon.org/sermons/1514.htm.

3. http://bible.crosswalk.com/Commentaries/ MatthewHenryComplete/mhc-com.cgi?book=lu&chapter=007.

4. Dorothy L. Sayers, *Are Women Human?* (Grand Rapids, MI: Eerdmans, 1971), 47.

5. Charles Spurgeon, "No Room for Christ in the Inn," *The Spurgeon Archive*, December 21, 1862, www.spurgeon.org/ sermons/0485.htm.

CHAPTER 12: PROOFS AND STATISTICS

1. Charles Spurgeon, "The Tender Mercy of Our God," *The Spurgeon Archive*, June 27, 1886, www.spurgeon.org/ sermons/1907.htm.

About the Author

Jen hails from Austin, Texas—a city and state that adore themselves. (If you're from anywhere else, please move here immediately and redeem the rest of your existence.) She has been married to her pastor husband, Brandon, for fourteen years, although she is only number seven on his speed dial (see chapter 3). However, he deserves much credit for remaining fiercely loyal to a woman who appeared on the six o'clock news talking about bird poop. Together, they have three children, who have taken them to the ER only twice to date, God love them. Gavin, Sydney Beth, and Caleb ensure that life will never be normal, whatever that is.

Jen and Brandon are starting a new church this year, living proof that God will use anyone. In a ridiculous turn of events, this is Jen's sixth book. God evidently has no standards. She travels nationally delivering sarcasm and truth to women everywhere. Jen's girlfriends represent her prayer team, support network, comic relief, and material, seeing how their lives are as obnoxious as hers. (You must have at least one vice and/or dysfunction to be her friend.) She speaks at several national conferences, which only indicates they don't research their speakers. She loves women so much, it's almost embarrassing. Jesus is her Hero, and the church is her passion. If you love any of those, call her.

You can reach Jen at www.jenhatmaker.com. She loves the local church and might even come to yours, as long as you're not like the Central Texas Women's Conference (see chapter 10).

Other exciting titles to help women with their spiritual growth.

Daughters of Eve

Virginia Stem Owens
ISBN-13: 978-1-60006-200-1
ISBN-10: 1-60006-200-8

Virginia Stem Owens invites you to examine some of the fascinating stories of biblical women. Some of these characters may be familiar to you; many you may have never heard of. As you learn about them, you may be surprised at what you learn about yourself.

Rewriting Your Emotional Script

Becky Harling
ISBN-13: 978-1-60006-188-2
ISBN-10: 1-60006-188-5

As a child who suffered sexual abuse, Becky Harling learned to live with an emotional script of shame, fear, and distrust. Determined to overcome her pain, Becky set out to rewrite the emotional script she had followed for years. In her second book, she invites women to let go of past hurts and redefine how they respond to life's emotional challenges.

Break Through

Marsha Crockett
ISBN-13: 978-160006-185-1
ISBN-10: 1-60006-185-0

Marsha Crockett knows the pain of a hard life. She invites you to search for the promise of God's power as you reconcile the reality of life with your faith. Through journal suggestions, Scripture meditation exercises, and practical tips, you'll learn how to move from stone-like hardness into a place of grace and truth.

To order copies, visit your local Christian bookstore, call NavPress at
1-800-366-7788, or log on to www.navpress.com.
To locate a Christian bookstore near you, call 1-800-991-7747.

NAVPRESS ⬤

Some kids dream of one day going to Harvard, Princeton or Yale. Some just dream of going to elementary.

America has always had a reputation for producing larger-than-life heroes. Now you can be one of them. Through a monthly tax-deductible donation to The Miracle Foundation, you can help the growing number of orphans in India with food, clothing, healthcare and textbooks so they can get an education and break the cycle of poverty once and for all. Add your name to the list of American heroes and make a child's dream come true.

The Miracle Foundation is empowering children to reach their full potential, one orphan at a time.

THE MIRACLE FOUNDATION

Be a hero. Sponsor an orphan.
www.miraclefoundation.org

Photo by Raime Banks – S.I.S./Choudwar Orphanage, Orissa, India